Penguin Books
Unfair to Goliath

Ephraim Kishon is considered to be Israel's national humorist, and his books and plays have spread his fame throughout the world. *Unfair to Goliath* is the fourth of his books to be published in Great Britain, and to appear in translation in almost every Western language. His plays, produced under his own direction, have had record runs in the Israeli theatre and have been performed on stage and television in other countries. His film *Sallah* has won many awards and was an Oscar nominee in 1965. He has been awarded the Israeli Nordau Prize and Herze Prize for literature and the Sokolov Prize for outstanding journalistic achievement. Born and educated in Budapest, Mr Kishon went to Israel in 1949 and now lives in Tel Aviv with his wife and three children.

Ephraim Kishon

Unfair to Goliath

Translated from the Hebrew
by Yohanau Goldman

Penguin Books

Penguin Books Ltd, Harmondsworth,
Middlesex, England
Penguin Books Australia Ltd, Ringwood,
Victoria, Australia

First published by André Deutsch 1968
Published in Penguin Books 1971
Copyright © Ephraim Kishon, 1968

Made and printed in Great Britain by
Cox & Wyman Ltd,
London, Reading & Fakenham
Set in Intertype Lectura

This book is sold subject to the condition that
it shall not, by way of trade or otherwise, be lent,
re-sold, hired out, or otherwise circulated without
the publisher's prior consent in any form of
binding or cover other than that in which it is
published and without a similar condition
including this condition being imposed on the
subsequent purchaser

This book is dedicated to all
nations which still have the ability
to laugh at themselves

Contents

'Corporal Goliath,' the military correspondents asked, 'how come that a giant like you, armed to the teeth, collapsed so quickly?'

'Because,' Goliath fumed, 'the bastard used unconventional weapons!'

It is a well-known fact that in a nation of pioneers there is a shortage of tradesmen. We read in the history books that the first settlers of North America were adventurers, criminals and prospectors, but there is no mention of a single plumber. This explains the strange situation in our country: we can defeat seven Arab armies, but are unable to fix a burst water main.

The Gemini Meet

No sooner had winter's chill started than a pipe burst in the wall of my studio and a dark-brown stain appeared on the plaster. I gave the pipe two days to mend its ways. Then, when the miracle did not materialize, I had no alternative but to appeal to our court plumber, the legendary Stucks.

The legendary Stucks lives in Holon and is what one may call elusive. All the same, on Saturday I nabbed him at the football field and he promised to come, provided I fetched him in my car before he went out to work – i.e., at 5.30 a.m. I asked him why did it have to be so early, didn't the job at my place count as work too, whereupon Stucks said no.

So I fetched him at 5.30. He barely glanced at the ever dampening wall and said:

'How can I get at the pipe? First a mason has to open the wall.'

With that he went, pointing out that now he had lost a whole working day. I was left by myself with the brown stain and a burning need for a mason. I didn't know any mason, where could I find one? I asked friends and acquaintances, neighbours, colleagues, but no one knew any mason (all right, James, hee-hee-hee). In the end someone whose brother is a contractor recommended Gideon, who is a handyman. That is, he repairs houses and lives not far from Bat Yam.

I located Gideon at the crack of dawn near the city gate, but he told me that he could come to our place only after work, at 9.00 p.m., so I fetched him at 9.00 p.m. Gideon glanced at the wall and said:

'How can I open the wall with water splashing out of the pipe? First the plumber should come and turn off the water.'

A slight shudder shook my frame. That's what I had been afraid of all along; deep in my heart I had known, but had tried to block out the unpleasant thought. Yes, they would have to be here together. Stucks could not attack the pipe without Gideon, and Gideon would get soaking wet without Stucks. Here were the real space twins, whose meeting could be brought about only at the cost of a gigantic logistic operation.

It is certainly easy to write down 'they'll have to meet' – the paper is very tolerant. But the very thought of the Stucks– Gideon summit was enough to give you the willies. Under our Levantine conditions the mating of Gemini 6 and 7 seemed child's play, since they were working according to the same time schedule, while in my case Stucks was free only mornings and Gideon evenings and salvation was nowhere in sight.

Twice I roamed the plains of Holon and three times the dunes of Bat Yam in order to coordinate the twins, but all my efforts aborted. The compromise I proposed between 9.00 p.m. and 5.30 a.m. – that is, to meet at my house at 1.15 a.m. – was rejected by both sides with indignant sibilants produced between tongue and incisors. Somewhat hesitantly I came up with the emergency solution of a Sabbath mini-desecration: Stucks agreed, but Gideon takes the kids out on Saturday – after all, he doesn't see them all week long. The rapidly expanding stain over my desk prompted me to try my luck again on the Holon–Bat Yam axis. On the day when, blue with cold, I burst into tears on Gideon's doorstep, the mason took pity on me and, pulling out a notebook from his pocket, went over the various possibilities.

'Look, sir,' he said in the end, 'Independence Day, April twenty-sixth, falls this year on a Monday. I think I'll tie it up with the Sabbath and won't work on Sunday either. So if that's all right with you . . .'

Shrieking with delight, I rushed over to Holon. Stucks then

took the wind out of my sails. He was certainly going to work on that Sunday, why shouldn't he work?

'Then what can we do, Stucks,' I said, 'what?'

Here – it was to be expected, wasn't it? – my personal Providence intervened. We found that on Tuesday night next (!) week the legendary Stucks was visiting his brother-in-law in Levontin Street and perhaps he could combine the visit with a blitz call on me, say at 7.30 p.m. Words failed to express my gratitude. Goodness, what a stroke of luck! A windfall! I drove like a madman to Bat Yam.

'Eureka!' I fell though Gideon's door. 'The plumber's coming on Tuesday night!'

'Sorry,' thus Gideon, 'I'm going to *The King and the Cobbler* on Tuesday.'

I almost fainted.

'Maybe,' I mumbled, broken-hearted, 'maybe you could go to the theatre on some other day. . . .'

'All right,' thus Gideon, 'but I'm not willing to run my feet off trying to change the tickets, if you don't mind.'

This remark was quite superfluous. Obviously I would go to the box office to change the tickets; after all, it was my wall on which the brown stain had reached ceiling level. In short: after labours which we have neither place nor time to describe, I succeeded in switching Gideon's two seats to December 26. I hurried straight to Bat Yam with the good news. Gideon's wife at once dashed my hopes: the twenty-sixth would not do. Grandma was bringing the kids back home. They were going to spend Hanukka with Grandma.

'Couldn't you,' I suggested, 'couldn't you bring the kids home one day earlier?'

'Why not?' Mrs Gideon allowed. 'Provided Grandma agrees.'

Grandma lives in Yokneam. A pleasant old lady, full of goodwill and helpfulness, but she does not travel on the Sabbath. And the twenty-fifth of December was a Sabbath.

'I'm not so religious myself,' Grandma said, 'but my late husband used to pray a great deal.'

And because of that my home would have to be turned into a swamp? I tried to convince the Old Lady of Yokneam that her sin would not be too heinous; what's more, if her husband were still alive he would certainly agree to get rid of the brats on Saturday, especially if someone came to fetch them back to the city by car and free of charge.

'No, no, sir,' the obstinate old lady persisted. 'I don't travel on the Sabbath, unless our Rabbi gives me a proper dispensation.'

The Rabbi was recuperating in a Zichron Yakov rest home. I found him walking in the garden for his pleasure.

'Venerable Rabbi,' I addressed him, 'if Grandma returns the kids on Saturday, Gideon can go to the theatre on the twenty-sixth of December and will be free for the Gemini meeting with the legendary Stucks next Tuesday at seven thirty. If this does not qualify as saving an endangered life, then I don't know what does.'

The Rabbi was an enlightened cleric. I donated a certain sum towards the erection of another yeshiva in Yokneam and the dispensation was duly made out, Grandma agreed, the kids, *The King*, 7.30. I drove to Stucks drunk with victory.

'Okay,' I shouted hoarsely, 'I've got a mason on Tuesday!'

'Sorry,' thus Stucks, 'the brother-in-law asked us to come on Wednesday.'

Yes, Stucks had even tried to ring me about the change but the phone had been engaged or something. It seemed the brother-in-law had forgotten that on Tuesday he had to go to a PTA meeting. The water stain had long ago spread to the ceiling.

'All right,' the brother-in-law allowed, 'provided you get them to move the PTA meeting to another day, why not?'

As a matter of fact, everybody was helpful, everybody was trying to help me. I hurried to the school director.

'Sorry,' that worthy said, 'we've already sent out the invitations.'

I went from house to house. Eighteen parents agreed right away to Thursday. Only four parents made difficulties, especially Mrs Plonit Winternitz, who had invited seven guests for Thursday night. Three of the guests agreed right away to switch over to Friday, but one of the objectors claimed he had no transportation on Friday, two women lacked baby-sitters and one had an arbitration meeting. I solved the transport problem by hiring a bus. My sister went to baby-sit for one of the women, the other woman I killed and buried in the garden. The arbitration was cancelled when I paid the fine.

So the PTA meeting took place on Thursday instead of Tuesday. The way was at long last open for Operation Gemini 8.

At 7.30 we were ready for the summit, the wall and I. We waited two hours, but no one came. At 11.00 p.m. Stucks showed up after having paid the visit to his brother-in-law. Where was the mason? Gideon, it transpired, had forgotten all about it.

Luckily it was no longer possible to distinguish the water stain, because the wall had disappeared, leaving only the stain – or, to be more precise, the whole wall had turned into a stain. So I quickly sold the apartment and bought a new one. Funny that this simple solution never occurred to me before.

The climate of our country is well ordered; one may even say it is a model of planning. Nine months of total summer, long-play sun without a trace of cloud, two transitional months and only one month of rain, and even that is mostly make-believe. Small wonder, therefore, that the umbrella has not yet penetrated into the consciousness of the population. I personally, former European that I am, sometimes go out with one. But I never come back with it.

Weather Forecast: Scattered Umbrellas

Possibly this mixed-up winter is to blame. Because you can't tell whether it's going to start at long last, or whether it's already over. The dark clouds gather and a Siberian wind howls in the streets – and fifteen minutes later the sun shines and the birds are twittering, and after two minutes it's again partly overcast with local showers. During these madcap times it's safer not to budge out of the house without an umbrella. That at least was the view of my little wife as I prepared to go and collect the car from Miko's garage.

'Take my umbrella,' the wife said, 'and for goodness' sake don't lose it!'

She repeats this warning like a parrot, every time I go out with an umbrella. It's a little ridiculous, really. What does she take me for – a kid?

'Tell me, my dear,' I asked her with succinct irony, 'when did I ever lose my umbrella?'

'Day before yesterday,' thus the wife. 'I beg you, don't lose mine as well!'

She gloats over the fact that the day before yesterday I forgot my umbrella somewhere. She is a great one at rubbing things in, the little one is. She exploits the fact that I have to go to Miko's garage with her umbrella. She is insulting me, really, because her umbrella is undeniably of the female gender: lean and blue, and on top, instead of a handle, it has a dog's head made of marble or something. I took hold of the loathsome freak with two fingers and went out into the pouring rain. It goes without saying that when I got off the bus the weather had turned completely summery. The skies were clear, the trees in bloom, nature was awakening, and I was walking on Dizengoff Street with a female umbrella. Naturally the car was not ready yet; Miko said it still had to be tuned up. On my way home I dropped in at the bank and withdrew some cash, then sat for a while at the California and talked with some friends about the crisis of theatre criticism. Then I hurried home because it was nearly 1.45.

The wife stood on the doorstep and asked:

'Where is the umbrella?'

Where was it? I had completely forgotten about it. But where had I forgotten it? Where? Think, man, the main thing was to keep a cool head.

'I left it at the California.' It came back in a flash. 'Of course, because I clearly remember that I held it between my knees so they wouldn't see it. That's it. I'll bring it, my dear, two minutes . . .'

I dashed straight to the bus stop through the rain which was falling again. Sitting in the bus, I mused on the British, who didn't walk a step without an umbrella and didn't lose it whenever the rain stopped, as a result of which that neat and orderly race had built itself an empire which was falling apart only now. In the grip of such international thoughts I arrived at my destination. I woke up at the very last minute, quickly jumped up, grabbed the umbrella and started pushing towards the exit.

'Hey, that's my umbrella!'

It was a very fat lady who had sat next to me all the time. Absent-mindedly I had taken her umbrella. Things like that happen. It had been lying practically under my hand; so I got a little mixed up, so what? The fat lady kicked up a big roar, called me pickpocket and other pet names. I explained to her that I didn't need her lousy umbrella, that I had several of my own scattered strategically all over town. In any case, I got off quickly and fled for my life. At the California I immediately found the wife's umbrella, or rather its debris. They had tossed it into a corner, trampled it underfoot and dirtied it into an abomination, the barbarians. My heart skipped a beat as I picked up the poor wretch. What would my little wife say? Life had become terribly difficult lately in this country.

'Well, you see,' I announced to the little one with forced gaiety as I came into the house, 'I found it!'

'What did you find?'

'Your umbrella.'

'This is my umbrella?'

It appeared that in the meantime they had sent back my wife's blue umbrella from the bank. Naturally, now I remembered, I had forgotten it at the bank. Of course it was at the bank. Then whose . . . whose . . . this black horror?

The telephone rang.

'This is the waiter from the California,' the waiter said, somewhat upset. 'They say here that you just walked in and picked up my umbrella. That's not nice. I finish at three and it's raining outside.'

'I beg your pardon,' I answered, greatly embarrassed, 'I'll return it right away!'

The wife was a little nervous.

'Take my umbrella,' she said, 'but for goodness' sake don't lose it!'

'What do I need your umbrella for? I've got the waiter's.'

'And on the way back, stupid?'

Has it ever happened to you, kind reader, that you walked in the street in the hot Mediterranean sunshine with two umbrellas on your arm, one of which was a black parachute and the other ended in a dog's head? It seemed to me that everyone in the bus queue was looking at me pityingly, their eyes saying 'Sissy!' I felt relieved when I started sneezing and could disappear into a nearby pharmacy to buy some aspirin. 'I won't go back into the street before it starts raining,' I vowed, but suddenly my stomach started rumbling, as I had not had my lunch, it will be remembered. I went to the corner buffet, ordered half a portion of falafel and wolfed it down in the bus. The waiter was waiting for me in front of the California. He looked somewhat disappointed.

'Listen,' he said, 'where is my umbrella?'

That is what he asked me, where was his umbrella. Do I know where your umbrella is, why ask me? And where is my wife's umbrella, you bastard? I almost threw myself on him. What's going on here, dammit, all the world's umbrellas get lost in my hands?

'What's the hurry?' I threw at the waiter. 'Ain't I here? You'll have your umbrella in a moment!'

I ran back to the bus in a heavy downpour. It's distressing, really. My wife's umbrella, all right, so I lost it, but the waiter's . . .

I burst breathlessly into the pharmacy.

'I left . . . here . . . a moment ago . . .'

'Yes,' the pharmacist said. 'Is this it?'

I grabbed the umbrella and dashed out into the street. To this day I could not swear that it was one of mine. It looked like my wife's, all right, yet I had my doubts. First of all, it was quite green, very short and ended in shiny ebony and a plaque: *To my sister, Dr Leah Pickler.* I'm afraid it was not my wife's. But I had to return something to the waiter, hadn't I? This is the survival of the fittest, my dear, today me, tomorrow you, it can't be helped. If you don't watch out, you are left sans umbrella before you can say 'Low pressure front.' It is said that at the Central Bus Station they distribute fresh umbrellas daily. You go and tell them: 'I lost my umbrella on Line 94.' 94 is a very busy line. 'Is this it?' a clerk asks. 'This is a rag,' you answer him. 'Show me something newer.'

'Hey, sir!'

The falafel vendor waved me cheerfully to his buffet. And you know what? Resting on his counter, like brother and sister, were the two wayward umbrellas – that of the California crook and that of my widow.

Three. A grand total of three.

Standing in line for the bus, I kept my eyes firmly glued to the ground. Dangling on my strong right arm were three umbrellas, a black one, a blue one and a green one. If at least it would rain! But no, the weather was very fine indeed, a light southwesterly breeze was blowing. I packed the three brollies into a bundle so as to give them a commercial look, as if I were an umbrella salesman or repairman or a collector headed for the Hobby Exhibition, but you cannot fool Jews. Some snotty brats hanging around the bus stop pointed me out and whispered among themselves amid primitive giggling. What sort of youth is this anyway?

In the bus I took a seat way back at the rear, hoping my triplets wouldn't be noticed. Thank goodness there were no comments, people had become used to me. Slowly – slowly I raised my glance and there ... facing me ... facing me ... facing me ...

Good Lord!

The fat lady. The same fat lady was sitting exactly in front of me. She fixed my umbrellas with a glassy stare and sneered:

'Had a busy day, eh?'

And without further ado she started explaining to her neighbours how she had caught me at noon. 'He simply picks up umbrellas and flees. Twenty years ago there were no such types in this country. A healthy young man, well dressed, and steals umbrellas, that's how he makes a living, shame on him.' Oblique glances were shot at me. 'Cop,' someone proposed, 'let's call a cop!' The crowd alarmed me, I don't like public appearances. At the next stop I jumped up, elbowed my way to the exit and threw myself into the powerful shower outside. As I picked myself up from the pavement I lifted my two hands beseechingly heavenward.

My two hands?

God ... on Line 5 ... three ... umbrellas ...

They are on their way to eternity.

I am standing in the downpour with closed eyes, like a present-day King Lear, and don't move. The water pours down my collar right through the soles of my shoes and purifies my sinful soul. Here I stand, from here there is no retreat, let the deluge come, let the whole world perish, I'm not moving from here until springtime.

The Jew's crooked mind, the anti-Semites claim, never rests. We are credited with many brilliant inventions, no one can deny it. I would like to present here a list of the latest, as proof that the time has come to take a brief rest.

Exercise at 3.45

We were sitting, Ervinke and me, staring at the demitasses in front of us. The time was 3.45, naturally p.m., and it was hanging like a dead weight on our minds. In the distance, Dizengoff Street was flowing raucously. A velocity-12 khamsin was blowing and the postmen had been on strike for the past fortnight. Nothing. The boredom was even worse than usual.

'Listen,' Ervinke finally mumbled, 'why don't they design cups for southpawed folks – that is, with the handle on the other side of the cup?'

'Do you think they care? Don't you know them? Sales is all they care about.'

'For five thousand years the same boring cups,' Ervinke sighed. 'Did they ever try to place the handle inside, so as not to disrupt the cup's outer wholeness?'

'Never,' I replied. 'Everything they do is routine.'

Ervinke raised the conventional cup to his lips and sipped.

'Just a little thought,' he fumed, 'just a little attention to details! Take pins. All over the world at least a hundred thousand people are getting pinpricks every hour. If they'd only manufacture pins with heads on both ends, nobody would prick himself.'

'Absolutely,' I said. 'That's just like toothless combs for baldheads.'

'I beg your pardon, but that's infantile.'

I fell silent. When I am insulted I clam up.

'This is no time for foolishness,' Ervinke chided me. 'I am discussing practical things. Like plastic dandruff. It's just come out. You scatter a little on your hair and that's that.'

'It will never look genuine.'

'No? You can look at it through a lens and you will never know the difference! We are living in a period of new materials, old boy. Ever seen a glass hat?'

'No,' I admitted. 'Why glass?'

'If you drop it, you don't have to bend down and pick it up.'

That sounded logical. It looked as if mankind was, after all, not marking time.

'What would you think of a cupboard,' I asked, 'with four legs on top as well?'

Ervinke looked at me, surprised. He always thinks I'm not too bright.

'Legs on top?' he mused. 'I see: if the top gets dusty, you simply turn the cupboard upside down.'

'Obvious.'

'These household things are very practical,' thus Ervinke. 'Take round handkerchiefs. I have been trying to get some for years.'

'You don't have to fold them, eh?'

'Right.'

'I've got something like that myself,' I confessed, blushing. 'I've even thought of taking out a patent on it.'

'Well?'

'A trouser traffic light. A miniature electronic instrument for the benefit of the well-dressed gentleman. If a button opens in your fly, a red light flashes and a buzzer sounds.'

Ervinke blinked, greatly perplexed. He had not credited me with such perspicacity.

'Your traffic light is too complicated,' he said in a voice hoarse with envy. 'It reminds me of the professor's cuckoo trap. You install it in front of the cuckoo clock's door, and when the bird comes out to blare its unnerving cuckoo, a small hammer hits it over the head and silences it for ever.'

'How many people in our country have cuckoo clocks?'

'Don't worry, there are plenty!'

There, now he is upset. I am sorry, but the whole idea of the cuckoo trap sounds silly from my end. If you don't want to hear the cuckoo, why not simply take the clock to a watchmaker and have him remove the bird? Why a trap? The ideas some people get, my word!

'Did you hear about the invention of the agronomist Michurin?' I asked Ervinke. 'Cross-breeding watermelons with fleas . . .'

'So that the seeds should pop out by themselves. A hoary old joke. Personally, I am more impressed by the cross-breeding of corn with a typewriter: while chewing the corn, as you reach the edge of the cob, it rings and jumps back and you can start on a new row.'

'Not bad.'

'Everything for comfort,' Ervinke allowed. 'I read somewhere that in the U.S. they have an advanced combine which plants potatoes all by itself, then automatically sprinkles them, cultivates them, picks them, washes them, peels them, cooks them and eats them.'

'Yes,' I remarked, smiling sadly. 'Man becomes superfluous. It's said they invented a computer in Japan which plays chess like a master.'

'I'd buy two,' Ervinke said, 'so they'd play chess at home while I could go to the movies.'

I paid and we went to the second show. Outside, an old beggar crouched, playing his transistor radio. The earth abideth forever, there is nothing new under the sun.

Of all the harsh legacies we inherited from our forefathers, none is harsher than the holy duty to engage in mass hospitality. If the good Yiddisher Tatte celebrates the bar mitzvah of his son or marries off his favourite daughter, he has to invite thousands of people he hardly knows and stuff them unconscious with food – or else run the risk of being called a miser. As a result, the happy parent generally ruins himself. On the other hand, he treats his guests to an evening they will never forget, try as they may.

A Twitch Out of the Past

It all started literally under the still-fresh wedding canopy of young Pomerantz. Preceding that, Dr Pomerantz had for days beseeched me over the phone to honour his son's wedding with my presence, as the young man had made his own participation almost conditional on my coming; and the bride, too, begged me to come, even if only for ten minutes. The whole affair was a pain in the neck. I hardly knew Dr Pomerantz. We had once met at the Yugoslav Ambassador's and discussed for a while my political cartoons, that was all. So what did I care about young Pomerantz's nuptials?

'Weddings are always dreadfully boring,' I complained to my wife. 'I don't know a soul there. It's idiotic, really. What shall I do?'

The little woman thought it over for a while, then her agile mind came up with the right solution:

'If you're invited, you have to go.'

Naturally, the wedding was exactly what I had expected it to be. It was obvious that Dr Pomerantz did not have the faintest idea who I was, his son absent-mindedly held out a limp hand, the bride not even that. Then we stormed the buffet – and that's where the man with the twitch entered my life.

That is to say, the man stood next to me and rhythmically twitched his face. He had a nervous tic or something. If I'm not mistaken, we didn't actually speak to each other except that he once asked me to pass the mustard, which I probably did. The only relief in the tedious evening came when the bridegroom accidentally spilled a glass of red wine over the bride's dress. I took advantage of the resultant commotion to flee into the fresh air. Before long I had forgotten the Pomerantzes, wedding and all.

About six months later I went to buy a lottery ticket and at the counter I bumped into another gentleman. While the lottery collector was using his scissors on my tickets, the gentleman looked at me and said:

'Well, how are the youngsters?'

I didn't know. 'Which youngsters, if I may ask?'

The man started twitching and that quickly refreshed my memory. Yes, it was the guy from the wedding of young Pomerantz.

'Haven't heard a thing about them,' I replied truthfully.

'Nor have I,' the twitcher retorted, 'but I seem to recall that the red wine was spilled all over the bride. . . .'

'Yes, yes, yes,' I agreed. 'Young Pomerantz did it. Well, let's hope everything's fine with them!'

With that, I quickly disengaged myself (the lottery ticket did not bring anything either). I hate to talk to people with whom there is not a subject in the world I can discuss. We had met at a wedding, fine, very nice, but that had been in the dim past; shall auld lang syne never be mercifully forgot? So I turned my back on the Twitch and erased him from my memory tape until that Sabbath when I entered a bus and sat down next to a faceless couple. For several stops we rode in deep silence, though I had at once recognized – no, sensed !– that I was again in the presence of my tormentor. In the grip of a nameless terror I counted the streets, hoping against hope to make the terminal without the need to go again into the painful details.

But fate had other designs. At the corner of Rambam my neighbour turned his head towards me and then I committed the worst error in my life. When he squinted at me, lightly twitching in the effort to place me, I couldn't stand the tension.

'Hi,' I blurted out, 'and how are they?'

So help me, the moment I said, 'And how are they,' an infallible intuition told me that he no longer remembered me and the wedding, and only I, in my criminal recklessness, had reminded him of events long past.

'Yes, yes, yes,' the man remembered. 'Pomerantz, or whatever their name was. Haven't seen them since. Meet my wife.'

I said, 'Pleased to meet you.' Twitch told her how we had met at Pomerantz's wedding.

'Remember,' he asked dreamily, 'how that wine . . .?'

'Yes – ' my face lighted up – 'was spilled.'

'Red wine, if I'm not mistaken.'

'It ruined the bride's dress.'

'So they are all right, you say?'

'I suppose so.'

'Nice to hear that.'

At this point the fascinating conversation came to an end; we fell silent because the only topic we could discuss was the by now not so young couple. Luckily we just then drew up in front of the terminal and the entire cast of the ghastly interlude dispersed.

Afterwards we again enjoyed a few years of relative quiet. I had practically forgotten the whole affair – until I boarded the train to Jerusalem.

It was fate. A cold shiver still runs down my spine whenever I recall that trip. I entered an almost empty compartment and draped my languid form across three seats. The train blew its whistle and started chugging, and I lifted my eyes and facing me . . . all alone with me . . . in the empty compartment . . . on the way to Jerusalem . . .

'Hee-hee-hee.' He twitched more than ever before. 'And how are the youngsters?'

I realized that he did not remember their names either.

'I dunno,' I answered, 'I never see them.'

'Nor do I.'

An ominous silence descended on the train. The wheels' clicking sounded like the knocking of the death beetle. It takes two hours to travel to Jerusalem. For the first time in my life I felt that my face was also twitching.

'The wine,' my companion whispered. 'The wine, remember?'

'Yes, the bride . . .'

'Red . . .'

'Spilled . . .'

'Pardon me,' I said and got up in a hurry. 'The dog!'

I dashed out of the compartment and elbowed my way to the last car. I stuck my burning brow out of the window, prohibition notwithstanding, and filled my lungs with fragrant mountain air. 'Why do I always have to talk to him about that?' I whined at the scenery which whisked by with typical Israeli nonchalance. 'Why can't we separate forever? Why must we torture each other all our lives because of an unhappy marriage?'

From then on I became cautious. I bought a car; at the café I always sat behind a pillar and I never, but never, went up to the capital. Once I spotted Twitch in the street, dashed into a doorway, sped up the stairs and hid in the laundry room on the roof. Because I clearly felt that if he once more asked me about the young couple, I would . . . I . . . I don't know what I was going to do.

Day before yesterday Nemesis caught up with me.

I took my son Raphael to *Festival on Ice*, and my parental duties made me neglect even the most elementary precautions. What happened? I sat down in my seat with Rafi squirming on my knees, and everything was nice and pleasant, and not only that, but in the darkness my effusive son struck up acquaintance with our neighbours and became particularly friendly with a boy his age who sat right next to us on his father's lap. I'm always happy when my son is social. I threw a contented glance to the right and saw that that boy . . . yes . . . he twitched . . . his face did.

For about an hour I did not dare to lift my eyes, but during the cruel intermission my worst fears were confirmed. The father was Twitch, all right. I feigned non-recognition, but this time it was he who broke down under the strain.

'Evening,' he whispered, his face pasty. 'Have you . . . heard . . . anything . . .?'

'For God's sake, the keys!' I shrieked and fled outside

behind a fat usher, trembling in every limb. My son had quite a job finding me.

'Dad,' he related, 'my new pal here says that his dad knows you. You were at a wedding. Is it true that they spilled red wine all over the bride?'

I stood there in the dusty square and uttered a mute lament. From now on the curse of the Pomerantzes would never again leave us. It would pass implacably from generation to generation, from sons to grandsons to great-grandsons, to the end of time.

Nothing is harder to bear than a moral debt, except a monetary debt. But a combination of the two is lethal.

The Hardest Currency

As a rule I keep a supply of ten-piastre coins in my pocket. On that morning, it had run out. I stood there in front of the cruel parking meter and scratched my head. Should a municipal inspector pass this way, the pleasure of his company would cost me five pounds. I tried to insert a twenty-five-piastre coin into the slot, but the meter would have none of it.

'Ten piastres?' I suddenly heard to starboard. 'Well, let's see . . .'

I turned in the direction of the voice and beheld Glick the engineer standing on the curb, fumbling in his pocket.

'Here you are!'

With that he fed the longed-for coin to the voracious parking meter. I did not know how to thank him. I offered him the twenty-five-piastre coin, but he would not accept it.

'Aw, come on,' he said, 'it's not worth mentioning!'

'Wait, I'll change it at the kiosk.'

'Stop it, will you! You'll find a way to reciprocate, I'm sure.'

And with that he left me with my thoughts and in a rather unpleasant situation. I don't like to be in anybody's debt. 'You'll find a way' – what way? What did he mean by that? Just to be on the safe side, I stopped at the florist's on my way home and sent Mrs Glick ten red carnations. That's how a gentleman behaves, if I'm not mistaken.

Why deny it, I expected the Glicks to give me a ring. Not

that I felt special thanks were due me for the flowers, but still. ... By nightfall there had been no call. I rang the florist. The flowers had gone by messenger at 4.30. What was going on? I could no longer stand the tension and rang the Glicks.

Glick himself came to the phone and we had a long talk on the port of Ashdod and on the new government and things like that. I stood it for fifteen minutes.

'By the way,' I said, 'did your wife get the flowers?'

'Yes. I think Eshkol should not give in to the pressure of the religious. After all, he received a clear mandate . . .'

And so on. I could feel my ears burning. Obviously, something had been very wrong with the flowers. When the tiresome conversation with Glick concluded, I related the whole affair to my spouse.

'But of course,' the little one said with finality. 'I, too, would have felt insulted. Who sends carnations nowadays? The cheapest flowers on the market.'

'But I sent ten.'

'Aw, stop it, you made a horrible impression. Now they'll take us for misers.'

I blushed. You can call me many names, but 'miser'? Next morning I went to the bookstore downstairs and bought Churchill's *History of the Second World War* in four very fat volumes indeed, and sent them to Glick the engineer.

There was no call by nightfall. The tension was well-nigh unbearable. Twice I dialled their number, but at the last moment replaced the receiver. Perhaps they did not realize that it was I who had sent the nice gift? 'Impossible,' the bookstore owner assured me, 'I clearly wrote that it was a gift from you.'

Two terrible days passed in nerve-racking silence. Then on Tuesday the books were returned with a terse note:

'Dear friend,' Glick the engineer wrote, 'when will you understand at long last that I don't expect any reward for the help I gave you on November 15, 1966? I did whatever I did out of good will and the desire to extend a helping hand to a fellow man in distress and that's all. I feel certain that you, too, would have acted in the same way. My reward is the wonderful feeling that I am still a human being in this jungle of selfishness and cruelty. Yours, Glick. P.S. I already have the Churchill.'

I read the letter to my wife in a faltering voice.

'Of course,' the little one said, 'some things simply cannot be paid with money. Sometimes, believe me, a small attention outweighs the most expensive gift. But you'll never understand that, I'm afraid.'

So I wouldn't understand what?

That very day I sent Glick our subscription ticket to the Philharmonic, first series.

On the night of the concert I lay in ambush at the corner of Huberman Street. Would he come? I hugged the wall and fingered the hoard of ten-piastre coins in my pocket. Yes, Glick came all right – with his wife. I went home genuinely relieved. I don't like to be in anybody's debt. For the first time in many days I could again relax. The phone rang at ten o'clock.

'We left in the middle,' Glick said in a hollow voice, 'the concert was awful.'

'I'm desolate,' I stuttered, 'I'm so sorry. ... I wanted to reciprocate for your nice gesture – '

'Ho-ho, old boy,' Glick interrupted me. 'Giving is an art! Don't think twice, don't make petty calculations, give with your whole heart. Never mind what, just give! Take myself, for instance! When on that day I saw what a desperate plight you were in at the parking meter, I could well have said to myself: "What business is this of yours! You have no car, you don't have to show solidarity with him. Pretend you never saw him and that's that!" But I'm not a designing person. "This man needs you," I said to myself and the purse was right there in my hand.'

I could literally feel myself wilting. Why, damn it, am I totally devoid of the faculty to make a nice gesture? Never mind what, just give, give . . .

'Glick is one hundred per cent right,' the little woman opined. 'You made such a mess of it that now only a dramatic step can save the situation.'

We racked our brains all day long. What to do? Buy them a cooperative apartment? Shares? Appoint them my sole heirs? In the end Glick's casual remark gave us a clue. How had he put it in his long monologue? 'I have no car,' he had said, if memory served me.

'I don't want to be left . . . without a car,' I mumbled dejectedly.

'That's typical,' the wife replied. 'Levantine!'

Our car was dispatched to the Glicks with two explanatory phrases: 'Bon voyage,' I wrote, 'and thanks again.'

This time their reaction was rewarding, though somewhat reserved.

'Morning,' he said, 'sorry to bother you, but I can't find the jack.'

The blood drained out of my face. The jack had been stolen more than a year ago and I had still not bought a new one! Now Glick would have a flat tyre somewhere on the road and curse me to the end of his days.

'I'm coming!' I yelled into the phone and hurried by taxi to buy a jack. I don't like to be in anybody's debt. So I drove straight to Jaffa, but suddenly on Rothschild Boulevard I came across my former car.

It was standing in front of a parking meter.

And next to the parking meter stood Glick the engineer, fumbling in his pockets.

With a hoarse shout I jumped out of the taxi and hurried over to the poor wretch.

'Ten piastres?' I inquired. 'Well, let's see . . .'

Glick turned round, stung. Blanching, he sobbed:

'Thanks! I don't need one! I've got one! I've got one! I've got one!'

And he went on feverishly rummaging in his pockets. Both of us were breathing heavily, because we realized only too well what was at stake. With shaking hands Glick turned all his pockets inside out, but did not find even a single ten-piastre coin. I shall never forget the hunted look in his eyes. With a slow and deliberate movement I inserted the coin into the pitiless slot:

'Here you are!'

Glick aged years in a matter of minutes. His back bent, he extracted the keys of the car and handed them over to me. He added the Philharmonic subscription, his eyes swimming in tears. By nightfall a bunch of flowers arrived for the wife. You have to hand it to Glick: he's a good loser.

Being a Jew is a profession, like being, say, a meteorologist. One has to keep making exact forecasts as to the direction from which lightning will strike tomorrow, with what intensity, what for, and isn't there some means of deflecting it at the last moment?

Good for Jews

'Well, sir, so justice triumphed after all.'

'Thank God.'

'Lyndon Johnson was elected President of the United States with an enormous majority, while Goldwater suffered an abject defeat. He got just thirty-nine per cent of the vote, only slightly more than our ruling party at the last elections here.'

'What a flop!'

'Indeed. Though we, as a people, don't have to be sorry. President Johnson is a loyal friend of our country, while Barry Goldwater always kept aloof from Israel, perhaps because of his Jewish grandfather.'

'That makes sense, psychology-wise. Really, how lucky we are that L.B.J. won.'

'I'm not so sure, sir. Quite possibly Johnson, whose friendship for Israel is quite well known, will now have to be somewhat severe towards us, so as to prove that the Jewish vote has no influence on his policy line.'

'Good Lord!'

'From that point of view, it is conceivable that Barry Goldwater's election would have been more favourable to us. Goldwater has been labelled anti-Israeli, so he would have had to make an effort to disprove this allegation. He might even have had to take the initiative in starting peace talks between ourselves and the Arabs.'

'So it's really a pity that they elected Johnson. As I understand it now, Goldwater would have been better for the Jews because he's against us.'

'Exactly. Though, had Goldwater made a gesture towards us, they might well have said that he was doing it because of his Jewish grandfather, and then he would have had to prove his outspokenly anti-Israeli feelings in order to set the record right. President Johnson, on the other hand, cannot harden his attitude towards us, lest it be charged that his friendship towards Israel was opportunistic, a trick for attracting the Jewish vote.'

'So Johnson is to be preferred after all?'

'I don't know. Goldwater is still nearer to us, because of his Jewish grandfather.'

'A pity Johnson had no such grandfather.'

'God forbid! So that he, too, should be against us?'

'I confess, I'm a little mixed up, sir. Couldn't you tell me in plain words: what's good for the Jews?'

'The United Jewish Appeal.'

The perspicacious reader certainly understood from an excellent previous story that in our country a Philharmonic Orchestra subscription is a first-rate status symbol. One may say that it is a matter of honour for anyone who can afford to buy his wife an evening dress from one of the exclusive dressmakers, or else is himself an exclusive dressmaker or an industrialist. Or has a successful export-import business. And a slight cold.

The Philharmonic Cough

Getting our subscription was child's play, really. Originally it had been bought by Mr S., director of the orchestra fund, who subsequently embezzled twenty thousand pounds and drew two years. With the bread-winner behind bars, hard times descended on Mrs S., and she found herself forced to auction off the orphaned subscription so as to pay her husband's debts, which ran into the thousands. The ticket passed to the exporter T.L., who bid sky-high because he did not hear the auctioneer, being stone-deaf. At the end of the very first season T.L. divorced his wife. Under the terms of the settlement the children stayed with the father, the subscription with the mother.

From here on, events took a criminal turn; that is, the former Mrs L. suddenly died, poisoned, and two months later her sub-tenant, a certain engineer G., was caught at the Mann Auditorium, suspiciously sitting in the deceased's seat. The ill-fated subscription was impounded by the Supreme Court and raffled off among the members of the Cabinet. (The Minister of Posts won.) So we did not get *that* subscription. But our neighbours, the Seligs, went abroad and left us theirs.

The beginning of the season's third concert was more or less routine. The players tuned their instruments (why can't they do it at home?), the conductor was given a warm ovation. He needed it badly, as the sudden winter storm howling outside had frozen all of us to the marrow. The conductor took the obligato bow as he stepped onstage, and the marvellous strains of Tchaikovsky's Pathétique filled the hall. The execution was not at all bad, but the concert really got under way only towards the end of the first movement. That is, during the reprise of the strings, from the front rows and the throat of a middle-aged knitted-goods manufacturer there suddenly came a sonorous cough. It was a sort of barking, sforzando cough, tempered by a certain amount of emotional tremolo, proof, if proof were needed, that the performer not only had a complete command of the throat-rasping technique but also possessed a tempestuous musical bent.

Obviously, this was the evening's real curtain-raiser.

The catarrhic middle rows and the sniffling sextets in the balcony, inspired by the clashing cadenza, joyously fell in with a throaty presto passage which filled the hall with an animated ensemble coughing of natural though nasal beauty, warmth and glow.

Outstanding in this passage was the owner of a well-known perfumery sitting near the aisle, who demonstrated an amazing virtuosity on her trumpet-like organ and produced mellifluous sordino effects through the adroit use of her handkerchief. The intonation of this accomplished soloist was somewhat brassy in spots, but breathtakingly precise, clear, factual and yet ... exciting. Her husband and accompanist, seated next to her, provided the contrapuntal motif with a limpid throat-clearing which sometimes bordered on the pathetic but was totally devoid of bathos.

These were moments of highest spiritual uplift. My neighbours, a somewhat reticent couple of fanatic music-lovers, coughed with exemplary consequentialness, interpreting the score lying open on their knees:

'Pam-pam' – tempo moderato cough. 'Pim-pim' – a molto vivace sneeze.

I sat there with the little one, listening raptly, though the orchestra onstage provided a jarring contrast to the harmonious tutti sneezing.

Undeniably, that je ne sais quoi which makes all the difference between an ordinary concert and an unforgettable evening was very much present in the hall.

The next item on the programme, a pallid Sibelius symphony, was somewhat drowned out by the polyphonic rattling of the ecstatic audience, but the total effect of organic oneness was complete. As for myself, I waited for a quarter's rest in the wheezing poem as the players filled their lungs in preparation for an extra flourish, and at the right moment rose somewhat in my seat, cleared my throat and let go with a recitative and highly expressive cough which revealed the sum total of my musical personality.

The effect was electrifying. Not only did the conductor beam at me, visibly pleased, and stop the orchestra lest it interfere with the concert out front, but he even cued the entrance of the soloist in the first row, a successful real-estate broker, who repeated the main theme in a hammering coda. Under the maestro's baton, the man produced remarkable bravura in sneezing. Bending double in his seat, he executed a series of expressive arpeggios on his crackling vocal cords, with the main theme taking on a more virile, martial timbre while the accompanying wheezes left his lungs in trills, by turns lyrically soft and raucously powerful, sometimes even shrill. It had been a long time since the Mann Auditorium resounded to such suggestive coughing, reminding one of a growling volcano erupting in a delicate Levantine miniature. The ensemble in the hall, despite its youthful vigour, felt itself carried away and yielded to this inimitable performer for whom the difficult art of concert coughing obviously held no secrets.

The well-selected programme ended with a crescendo on the gamut of unison coughing, a piece of unexcelled authenticity leaving no room for phoney romanticism but offering practically boundless scope for individual snorts and the display of utmost instrumental virtuosity on handkerchiefs, scarves, neckties and inhalation apparati.

An impressive evening of spectacular works and flawless performance.

I've said somewhere in this book that we are very much tradition-bound, or, rather, that tradition is holding us in an iron grip. Take, for instance, that Highest Commandment from the Book of Books which enjoins us not to work our land once every seven years. What is to be done? If we leave the land to lie fallow, we shall starve. If we work it, we shall provoke the Almighty. Compromise, let's compromise, for God's sake.

Shmitta Year

The High Regions are shining with immaculate light and the Place radiates brilliance. Silence and majesty reign in Space. The Lord is sitting there, placidly quiet as always when the Work is being obediently carried out according to His wishes. And then, an audience is requested by one of the officials, a nervous little imp with a sparse beard.

'Lord of the World,' he starts self-importantly, 'it's about Israel again.'

The Lord waves resignedly.

'I know, the non-Kosher meat preserves from Argentina . . .'

'If it were only that,' the official sighs hypocritically. 'Master of the World! They are working the land in the kibbutzim of the religious parties.'

'Never mind,' thus the Lord, 'it won't hurt them.'

The Retinue draws closer.

'O King,' the official whispers. 'It's a shmitta year, the seventh year, Lord of the World, when the land rests, so that Your will may be fulfilled.'

The Lord closes His eyes, thinks. The Light dims, the Word reverberates a hundred times in Space.

'I see! So they work the land which I gave them, they work on the Sabbath of rest, though I had forbidden it to them. They are again at it! Where is Fried?'

Panic and confusion. Messengers fly in all directions, looking for the representative of the Religious Front in Heaven,

Adelbert Fried, formerly of Bratislava. Lightning flashes in space.

Adelbert Fried arrives at a run, his prayer shawl floating after him.

'Why do you work your fields in the seventh year?' the Lord thunders. 'Answer.'

Adelbert Fried shrinks to about half his size. In his embarrassment he plays with his skullcap.

'Lord of Hosts,' he says, 'we don't work our land. We have no land whatsoever in Israel.'

'What sort of nonsense is this! What's the matter with your land?'

'The Rabbinate sold it to an Arab. They sold the whole country. There is no land in Jewish hands anywhere in Israel, so you see that's why it can be worked.'

The Lord frowns heavily.

'Sold it to an Arab? All of Israel? Where's my legal adviser?'

Dr Benjamini is already floating before the throne.

'Master of the World!' he explains. 'The situation is as follows. The Ministry of Religions, on the strength of a written power of attorney issued by the Ministry of Agriculture, has contractually sold all Israel lands for a period of one year to an Arab. The contract was signed in Jerusalem, in the presence of Government and Rabbinate representatives, on the date of Av Yud Zayin.'

'When is that?'

'About the middle of August.'

Deep furrows appear on the Lord's brow.

'So they had to sell the land during the shmitta year, of all times, and for exactly one year. Sell all of Israel to an Arab? A strange coincidence . . .'

'The contract, duly signed and sealed, was placed in a bank safe,' Dr Benjamini continued. 'Legally it's absolutely watertight.'

'Did they blow the ram's horn?' the Lord asks.

'Of course,' Adelbert Fried says, 'of course.'

The Lord is not yet convinced. The Retinue cowers whimpering, the wind chases stormclouds.

'I don't like the look of things. I ordered that the land should rest in the seventh year and the farmer should also rest. I never said that this command should not refer to sold land.'

'I'm very sorry, Highest Lord – ' Adelbert Fried falls to the ground – 'strike me if You wish, but I remember this better than You do. You gave explicit orders.'

'I? Where are the minutes?'

'Moses! Moses!' A bidding voice floats through Space until Moses finally appears from beyond the Spheres. In his hands he carries the five books of minutes.

'Read me the relevant parts, son!'

'My third book, twenty-fifth chapter,' Moses reads. "Speak unto the children of Israel and say unto them, When ye come into the land which I give you, then shall the land keep a sabbath unto the Lord." '

'See?' the Lord says. 'I told you.'

' "Six years thou shalt sow thy field, and six years thou shalt prune thy vineyard, and gather in the fruit thereof." '

'You see, King of Kings,' Adelbert Fried remarks. ' "Thy field" – therefore the command does not refer to the land of *others*.'

The Lord is angry. 'I didn't say at the time anything about "thy land".'

'Lord of the World,' Fried insists, 'this text was approved even by the Rabbinical Grand Council of Agudat Israel.'

The Lord looks up. 'Did they blow the ram's horn?'

'Of course.'

'Hm . . .'

The Retinue sighs, relieved. The Lord, Blessed be His Name, has apparently accepted the arrangement. Tension lessens, the Light spreads in Space. But no! The Lord's face darkens, His features show traces of anger.

'Say what you like,' the Voice falls on those present, 'you won't convince me. You are cheating me somewhere, only I don't quite know where.'

'Lord,' Adelbert Fried whispers, 'Lord . . .'

'Quiet! So you say the Ministry of Religions was empowered by the Ministry of Agriculture?'

'In writing, Lord, in writing.'

'Even then, how can a Ministry have such jurisdiction? To sell my country to an Arab? My Israel? For how much did they sell it?'

'For fifty pounds,' Dr Benjamini whispers, with lowered lids. 'And even that was received by the Arab.'

'Things are getting fishier and fishier. Who ever heard of such a thing? The land which I gave forever to Abraham's nation is wasted by a profane, tottering Minister of Agriculture ...'

'They even blew the ram's horn,' Adelbert Fried whispers apologetically, but even that does not help now. The Voice rings like a brazen bell, thunder crashes through Space, the trumpet of the Spheres sounds below.

The Lord rises.

'I've decided,' says the Judgement. 'I'm raising a formal objection.'

Lest we forget, we just had a brief war against 110,000,000 Arabs who yearned to carry out our slaughter, long overdue. We, on our part, blundered abysmally, and again defeated them. The world, following with bated breath our struggle for survival, suddenly came alive to the plight of the victims of those 2,000,000 Jewish aggressors. On TV screens and in the world press arose the indignant cackling of objective foreign observers.

Unfair to Goliath

Now, a month after a shameful chapter in Israel's history has come to a close, this political commentator feels that the time is ripe for a more objective appraisal of events. The facts are well known: after extensive manoeuvring on both sides, the Philistine camp was pitched facing the Israel army at Shochon, the battle array creating a great amount of tension. In these critical moments Second Lieutenant Goliath went out and stood between the two camps and raised his voice to prevent unnecessary bloodshed. His challenge was taken up by an Israeli fighter, a renowned lion hunter named David, who carried out a surprise attack on his opponent and brutally butchered him.

So much for the facts. From a purely military point of view, the efficacy of the operation cannot be denied; but from a moral viewpoint, we may well ask David, and those who sent him, a number of pertinent questions. We hasten to add that in debunking this nascent myth we are not guided by hatred for the people of Israel; quite on the contrary, we are attempting to remove a heavy blemish on the name of this restless tribe.

We are not of the opinion that in a duel among soldiers an absolute balance in armaments and ability must prevail. But as a matter of elementary decency and fairness, there must be at least a modicum of equality between the combatants.

We are sorry to say that in the fight between David and Goliath, the scales were heavily weighted in favour of the former. First, as far as equipment was concerned: while Goliath was encumbered with a brass helmet, a coat of mail, a shield, a sword and a spear, the total weight of which was more than sixty kilograms, David enjoyed superior mobility due to the light arms at his disposal. In addition, Goliath's unfortunate size gave his ponderous body a height of four metres and made it quite impossible for him to come to grips with the sturdily built Israeli fighter. Add to this the tactical superiority engendered by the surprise attack, and one may say quite confidently that David's victory was a foregone conclusion.

It may be assumed that historians will go on arguing who started this disgraceful fight. It is a fact that for the forty days preceding the battle there was no change whatsoever in the array of the two armies; in fact, towards the end a certain détente made itself felt which raised hope for a settlement through diplomatic action. Besides, the most reliable reports available clearly state that Goliath just 'arose and came and drew nigh' to meet his opponent, while David was already running furiously towards him, a fact which leaves little doubt as to the identity of the aggressor. To cut short any fatuous arguments, we would like to quote here the testimony of Second Lieutenant Goliath's armour bearer, who is only now recovering from the effects of blast caused by the collapse behind his back of his heavy master.

'Goliath made a point of never attacking first,' the armour bearer said. 'He was a kind man, full of humour and joie de vivre. Many people think that he was a coarse warrior, but in fact his was a poet's soul and he played the violin very nicely. I can still see him sitting of a night at the campfire, singing that song he loved above all others: "Jews have pity on me, I've no father, no mother . . ." Because Lieutenant Goliath was an orphan, and his excessive height had caused him a great deal of suffering in childhood. What he hated most in life was blows and fighting. I'm convinced that he would have worked out a compromise even with that kike and had cursed his God just for domestic consumption. His hobby was birdwatching, he was a great animal lover . . . but now . . . all this . . . is gone . .'

In glaring contrast with the naïveness of the country boy, there is the cold-blooded planning of his smart city-dweller opponent, who demanded his wages even before the fight: 'What shall be done to the man that killeth this Philistine?' Pragmatic David built his victory on the use of unconventional arms, which he painstakingly gathered out of the brook over a long period of time. And if credence is to be given to his pre-hostility bragging, he even counted on assistance from above.

The fight itself certainly adds no glory to the Israeli nation. According to the Philistine eyewitnesses, David behaved in a shameful way – to use moderate language. It is hard to forget the figure of the hysterical bully rushing with obscene shouts towards his well-bred, helpless opponent, taking his sword and bringing it down again and again, with pathological, murderous lust, his comrades on the hills all around meanwhile rending the air with ear-splitting shouts. The shocking spectacle of the slaying of a wounded man lying on the ground, the disgusting cruelty with which the head was severed – all this barbarous handiwork leaves no doubt as to David's fighting standards.

It is then not surprising that David's first act after the callous slaughter was the 'collection' of his fallen opponent's arms, and their conveyance to Jerusalem, together with a substantial amount of plunder his comrades had gathered in the abandoned camp of the Philistines. This unbridled lawlessness may possibly be excused by the fact that the Israel soldiery were flushed with victory and easy territorial gains, but as neutral international observers, we may not disregard the human aspect of the affair, an aspect where the vanquished Philistines clearly carried the day. The figure of Second Lieutenant Goliath is doubtless one of the most tragic in the annals of armed conflict. The Philistine freedom fighter fell, overwhelmed in a battle lost even before it was joined. Lying on his back on the battlefield, beaten and humiliated, his blue eyes seemed to be raising a mute accusation at the unfeeling skies:

'Why? Why . . .?'

His widow, Mrs Frederika Goliath, has not yet recovered

from the heavy blow, as you can all see on the TV screen. The fourteen children clinging to her skirts are the orphans of the brave officer, who had naïvely believed that the time had come to liberate occupied Palestine.

'We were left without a father and husband,' Mrs Frederika Goliath is saying quietly, fighting back her tears. 'It is very hard for me to make ends meet, now that we are left without a breadwinner, especially since all my husband's personal possessions were stolen by the rowdy. I'm not complaining, I try not to cry, but when the little children keep asking me, "Where's Daddy Goliath, has he killed all the Jews yet?" my heart, my mother's heart, is breaking. The murderers did not even return my husband's body, the world is indifferent and didn't even raise a finger.'

We lowered our eyes before the widow's heartrending plaint. The wheels of history have overrun the small Philistine nation, dear viewers. David's victory is complete, his military superiority indisputable, but this is the victory of brute force over the highest spiritual values. Second Lieutenant Goliath, victim of brazen aggression, has entered the pages of history as a symbol of the little man facing the relentless juggernaut of war.

Now that the war is over, and the best forces of the government are engaged in the international arena, this writer would like to reminisce on the quasi-messianic days through which our country went during Operation Beat-the-Hell-out-of-Them.

Those Were the Days

The sharp turn in the character traits of our people started, if we are not mistaken, with the removal of the U.N. Force from the Strip. During those marvellous days one noticed that on the country's highways, in the shadow of the traffic lights, car owners were no longer shooting murderous glances at their fellow drivers; quite the contrary, here and there one experienced a friendly flickering of familial affinity.

'Hi,' the glances said, 'we're all in the same boat, aren't we?'

And from then on, every rash step of Gamal's brought out another of the nation's long-dormant qualities. Politeness, good manners and graciousness spread like wildfire. Neighbours suddenly started talking to each other. At the grocery the tenor was as cultured as could be:

'Please, ma'am, you came first, if I'm not mistaken.'

'What does it matter, sir, aren't we all Jews?'

And we loved our fellow man at least as much as we loved ourselves. By the time Hussi of the miraculous instinct flew to Cairo for the signing, perfect strangers were walking the streets arm in arm. We admired the fire brigade and the assessing officer, we loved the traffic cop fulfilling his arduous duties under difficult conditions. We were good in those days. We were also quiet, talked in whispers and walked on tiptoe as befits the People of the Book. If someone dared to sneeze in public, reproachful eyes were turned on him:

'Now? When the Iraqis move into Jordan?'

We had some moments of greatness. It is said that in the north of Tel Aviv mysterious people paid back nonexistent debts. Unknown boys went out to dig never mind what, their sisters became air-raid wardens and their mothers were nurses. On the Saturday when de Gaulle came out with the spare-parts bit, you couldn't buy cinema tickets in Jaffa because everybody at the box office was claiming that the other fellow was before him in the queue.

And the hitch-hiking – oh boy!

The language is quite inadequate for doing justice to the subject. On the first day of the war, before even Comrade Kosygin knew that the Egyptian Air Force had been grounded for good, you could see city drivers literally hunting lonely soldiers to offer them rides. In the air-raid shelters anyone who did not have at least two paratroopers to his credit was ostracized. Car owners gave preference to elderly ladies with glasses, so as to remove any doubt as to their honourable intentions.

But after the fall of Gaza, they already wouldn't take fat ones. And after the capture of Ramallah, men with haversacks were out. During the liberation of the Syrian ridge, only special hardship cases were getting rides. And today the old Mediterranean style is back in fashion.

Yesterday, a driver whom we tried to overtake on the curve shouted at us:

'Hey, where's the fire, you bloody fool!'

'Hey yourself,' we roared back, 'Nasser's getting MIGs!'

'Go ahead, sir,' thus the man, 'I've got plenty of time.'

In other words, the time is not yet quite ripe for a complete normalization. The Camp of Peace has set up tents in Cairo and our new Ministry of Minorities is at present handling the Jewish population. So the emergency of good manners continues until further notice.

One may say many negative things about our Arab neighbours, but one has to admit that they are on the way to becoming perfectly organized. Countries in which only a few years ago there reigned utter anarchy, today have a planned economy worked out down to the last assassination.

A Matter of Planning

'President Abdul Rahman, permit me to congratulate you on behalf of my paper upon becoming head of the Iraqi Republic. Our readers would be most grateful if you could tell them something about your plans for the future.'

'I have not yet worked out a detailed time schedule for myself. In any case, I'll devote the next few months to the strengthening of national unity. In a week's time I shall announce a general amnesty for Communists and thereby I hope to remove all the obstacles in the way of achieving Socialism.'

'And in the economic field, Mr President?'

'A fuller exploitation of our national resources and a revision of the contracts with foreign oil companies. The immediate ending of hostilities against the Kurds ought to generate stability and a proper climate for the introduction of reforms in the educational system. By the middle of June I hope to implement these plans.'

'Why by the middle of June, if I may ask?'

'Because then I'll uncover the first plot against my régime.'

'General Staff officers?'

'No. For once the plot will be hatched by the Garrison Commander of the Northern Region, one of my most trusted comrades. As a matter of fact, I'll promote him to Brigadier General in two weeks' time.'

'Will the plot succeed?'

'No. The Garrison Commander's brother will squeal to the Secret Police. Following this, I'll naturally carry out a ruthless purge of the officer corps, together with extensive arrests of Communists. I'll hang the leader of the rebels with my own hands. But this is off the record.'

'Of course, Mr President. When will the purges end?'

'By August, I hope. On the twentieth of that month I'm flying to Cairo for talks with Abdul Nasser on the unification of the two sister states and the liberation of Palestine.'

'So, at the end of August we'll unite with Egypt, Mr President?'

'Alas, no. While addressing the cadets, I'll be fired on by a medium sub-machine gun.'

'Allah!'

'Tut-tut-tut. Only the Minister of Defence and the Commander of the Sixth Divison will be gathered to their fathers. I shall be only nicked in the shoulder and broadcast a speech to the nation from my hospital bed. I'm already working on this speech and shall record it in a few days so that it will be ready in good time.'

'May I know the contents of the speech, Mr President?'

'I'll thank Allah for saving both myself and Iraq, and announce a country-wide purge of the pro-Egyptian officer corps who organized the plot while I was engaged in talks in Cairo. The Commander of the Armoured Corps will support me, and in the middle of September I'll appoint him my Deputy. In November I'll deeply regret this, but by then it will be too late.'

'And until then, Mr President?'

'Until then, nationalization of the banks and a massacre of leftists. I'll broadcast the public trial and hanging of nine Communist leaders on TV.'

'May I ask, with your own hands?'

'Not this time. Just then I'll be in Moscow, negotiating the purchase of a large shipment of the latest Soviet arms. The Deputy Chief of Staff will accompany me.'

'Not the Chief of Staff, Mr President?'

'No. He'll be involved in an attempt on my life in the first week of October.'

'Shots?'

'No, bombing. The Commander of the Air Force takes advantage of the renewed fighting against the Kurds and on the morning of October ninth bombs my house.'

'Is your body found under the debris, Mr President?'

'Not yet. According to my plan, I'll miraculously escape with my life. I'll be in the basement at the time the bombs shatter my study. The chair you are sitting on now and the bookshelf will be smashed to bits.'

'So, on the ninth of October . . .'

'Yes. Naturally, delays of a day or two are always possible, but I don't think my timetable will change materially. As a matter of fact, wait — it's all written down here in this notebook. In the middle of October I have purges. Then, more purges. Towards the end of the month the Minister of Education is executed.'

'Plot?'

'No, mistake. Then I have a few big massacres. A curfew. Another curfew. Closing down of all shops. The Governor of the Southern District is arrested. On November first, goodwill mission from the United States. Plot of the new Minister of Defence is foiled.'

'When is the overthrow, if I may ask, Mr President?'

'According to plan, my overthrow is scheduled to come between the eighth and the eleventh of November.'

'The Deputy Chief of Staff.'

'Yes, he'll also be involved, but the real leader will be my Deputy, the Commander of the Armoured Corps, whom I had rashly appointed in September.'

'I got that. What exactly is going to happen, if I may ask?'

'Feigning routine manoeuvres, the Mechanized Division will capture the radio station and my cousin, who will be appointed Minister of the Interior late in October and broadcast an appeal to the nation in which he'll call me a . . . Walt, where did I write it down? . . . Yes, he'll call me "a rabid dog with bloodstained fangs". He'll also broadcast a call for national unity.'

'Very reasonable, Mr President. May I ask, why don't you

order the blowing up of the radio station before the rebels can capture it, since you know the exact dates?'

'Of course I'll issue such an order. But my trusted man, the Garrison Commander who is responsible for the radio station, will join the rebels.'

'I see. Will you fight, Mr President?'

'No. I'll flee in my striped blue pyjamas. According to my reckoning, they'll catch me two days later disguised as a woman, in the outskirts of Baghdad, after which they'll chop off my head.'

'Will your body be dragged?'

'Naturally. The length of the main streets.'

'Your plans for the more distant future, Mr President?'

'Here, approximately, I see my mission as President ended and completed.'

'And who'll be the next President, if I may?'

'In my testament I'll recommend the same Garrison Commander who will later on betray me.'

'What are his plans?'

'National unity, I suppose. But perhaps you better contact him personally around November fifteenth. I'm responsible only for my own timetable. And excuse me, I have to hurry to the victory parade.'

'Thank you very much, Mr President.'

A very special problem is posed by the Jews still living in the Arab countries. It must be somewhat odd for the Jews living in Cairo to pray at Passover: 'Blessed be the Lord Almighty who took us out of Egypt, the Land of Bondage'. Small wonder if they are a little mixed-up.

François the Bridgehead

Our dramatic meeting with the sheikh, the son of the burning desert, took place some years ago in a small restaurant on the Avenue MacMahon, not far from the Arc de Triomphe. We had dropped in at the restaurant quite by chance, because in Paris every restaurant is 'the best', but had some difficulty deciphering the menu with its curlicued Gallic expressions. We therefore asked the waiter to tell us about one of the dishes which had a long name ending in Marie Antoinette. This set off some rapid-fire French chatter of which, to our chagrin, we did not understand a syllable. We were sitting there on the verge of despair when suddenly we heard in excellent Hebrew:

'It's simply a cold plate.'

Greatly surprised, we looked at the man at the next table. He was a quiet, middle-aged gentleman, very well dressed, though somewhat swarthy. His behaviour was rather strange: after his brief remark he went back to his meal, completely ignoring us. The wife and I exchanged puzzled glances.

'Pardon me,' I finally addressed the stranger, 'are you an Israeli?'

'No,' he answered, 'I'm an Arab.'

And he went on eating. The salt herring stuck in my wife's throat and I felt goose pimples forming on my skin. Small wonder: for the first time face to face with the enemy! Here we were sitting in the heart of Paris peacefully chewing a cold plate, and who knew but tomorrow we might look at each other over the sights of our rifles?

My inborn chivalry told me it was only fair to show him the respect due to a valiant opponent facing certain defeat.

'A-salaam Aleikhum.'

'Aleikhum a-salaam.'

The little one and I stopped eating, so excited were we. Were we allowed to speak to him at all? Maybe he was the agent of a foreign power trying to ferret military secrets out of us and therefore he was doing his best to win our confidence by telling us he was an Arab. But no! The man was calm and collected, his noble features were highlighted by horn-rimmed glasses riding on his eagle's-beak nose. His eyes reflected the wide open spaces this freedom-loving son of the desert had roamed. He must be a sheikh or something.

'Are you, sir, from Isr . . . Palestine?'

'No, I'm from Lebanon.'

Tension dropped somewhat. Second-league. But at least he was not a Syrian, Allah be praised.

'I lived in your country for many years,' the sheikh added in flawless Hebrew. 'Before the war.'

We lowered our eyes, greatly embarrassed. Maybe he had left behind his house, his lands? I gathered my courage and made a gesture of goodwill towards the unhappy refugee.

'I pray,' thus I, 'that the day shall come when we shall again be able to visit each other's countries.'

'Let's hope,' the sheikh answered. 'Peace will be to the benefit of all.'

'We have no greater desire than to come to an understanding with the Arab nations.'

'Let's wait and see.'

The climate was one of cordial coexistence. A most pleasant surprise, so help me. At home they stuffed us with all sorts of stories of burning hatred, etc., and here the sheikh was talking as if he were one of ours.

'We don't know who will be the first to sign the peace with Israel,' I remarked, a meaningful smile on my lips, 'but we know for sure that Lebanon will be the next one.'

The shadow of a smile flashed over the sheikh's face.

'Could be. Though the Arabs are unable to make peace even among themselves.'

'The Arab states,' I came to the defence of our good neighbours, 'are in a phase of national awakening and consolidation of independent patterns.'

'The hell they are,' said the sheikh. 'They simply can't get along, that's all.'

No use denying it: we were flabbergasted. We had never expected such detachment, such objectivity from the king of the desert. 'Listen,' the woman whispered, 'he must be a Christian.' Yes, that was likely, they are more moderate.

'In your country, sir,' I said, 'the majority of the population belong to the Christian faith, don't they?'

'Not quite.'

'Are you Catholic, sir?'

'No.'

'So you are a Moslem?'

'No.'

'Then what are you?'

'What do you mean, what am I? I'm Jewish.'

I couldn't see myself, but the wife's face was symptomatic of an involved brain short-circuit. She temporarily even squinted.

'Excuse me,' I mumbled, 'you are Jewish, sir?'

'What else did you expect?'

The blood rushed to my head.

'Listen, Yankele,' I roared, 'then why do you let me chatter here about peace among our peoples? Why didn't you say right away that you are Jewish?'

'You didn't ask.'

'I asked!'

'You asked whether I was from Palestine. I'm from Lebanon.'

'But, for God's sake, you are not an Arab!'

'Why not?'

I started foaming at the mouth. How dare he ask me to take him for an Arab? One only had to look at his crooked Jewish nose and bleary eyes to realize that his forefathers and mine had come out of Egypt in the same convoy.

'You are not an Arab, old boy,' I said to him, 'because you won't fight against Israel!'

'We are exempted from military service,' the sheikh agreed and added: 'But apart from that, we are full-fledged citizens.'

Before long we learned that in Lebanon there are about nine thousand Jews who enjoy full equality and freedom, except in the field of transferring foreign currency abroad. They may be anything they like except soldiers, clerks, judges, policemen, politicians, teachers, farmers, sportsmen, lawyers, journalists, radio announcers and muezzins.

'So what profession is open for you?'

'Brushes.'

He, too, manufactured brushes. He had two factories in Beirut and a branch office in Paris. Half the time he spent at home and half in France, and what floored me was that his name, too, was Ephraim.

'But,' he said, 'they call me François.'

'That's what they called me, too, back in the old country.'

That called for a round of drinks. Froike told us how he did business with the Egyptians. Twice he had gone to Cairo and twice the Egyptians had arrested him, but both times they had released him and let him carry on his business. In the fall he would again go there to be arrested. He has a lot of Arab friends at home. I asked him, how did he talk about Israel to them? Froike replied that they steered clear of the subject. I insisted: 'Still?' he retorted: 'Still, nothing.

'But I have relatives in Haifa,' he boasted. 'Though I can't write to them.'

'So why don't you come for a visit?'

'They might find out and not let me return to Lebanon.'

'So what? So you'll stay in Israel.'

François fidgeted about in his chair, sweating profusely.

'Well,' he said, 'we in Lebanon are serving as a sort of bridgehead to a rapprochement between Jews and Arabs.'

With that, the sheikh got up, looked round stealthily and quickly took leave. 'Shalom Ephraim,' I whispered to him, 'next year in Jerusalem.' I think he nodded his head in assent. But we haven't met since then. Though we took the city for him.

A question which perennially crops up: how does it feel to live in a country where all are brethren? That is where the Minister of Defence is a Jew, the Chief Justice is a Jew, and the traffic cop is also a Jew. And indeed, especially with the latter, it is a pleasant feeling to know that the traffic ticket was not written out by some alien goy, but by our own flesh and blood, by our brother, the traffic cop. Unavoidably, here and there, a little fratricide is practised all the same.

A Free Ticket

Gusts of hot desert winds swept dunes of sand on to the sidewalks. The coffee, on the other hand, was weak and luke-warm. Through the plate-glass window of the café Ervinke watched the fight for survival going on outside. It was a hum-drum day, in no way different from yesterday or the day before that. The groans of much-tried drivers rose high to the heavens, but their laments broke against the rock-like indifference of the traffic cops.

'Enough,' Ervinke said and jumped up, 'let's go on a police action!'

I paid and we made a beeline for the nearest police station. Ervinke asked the desk officer:

'Where can I report a traffic offence?'

'Here,' the officer answered. 'What's happened, sir?'

'I drove my car down Shlomo Hamelech Street,' Ervinke opened, 'and parked it at the corner of King George.'

'Yes,' the officer said, 'I'm listening. What happened next, sir?'

'I drove off.'

'You drove off?'

'Yes, I drove off and almost forgot the whole thing. But then I happened to pass the scene of the crime, and suddenly it flashed through my brain: "Good Lord, the stop!"'

'What stop?'

'The bus stop! Don't you know that there is a bus stop at the corner of Shlomo Hamelech and King George? Officer!

I'm almost certain that I parked less than twelve metres from it!'

The officer blinked his eyes.

'Is that why you came here, sir?'

'Yes.' Ervinke broke down. 'At first I didn't want to do anything about it. "You parked for only half an hour," I told myself, "no one saw you, what do you care?" But then my conscience began to plague me. I went back to Shlomo Hamelech Street and checked the distance in steps. It was nine metres at the most! I realized that I'd never regain my peace of mind except by surrendering to the police. And now I'm here.' Ervinke wound up his confession and pointed to me. 'This is my counsel.'

'Hello,' the officer said and shrank away from his desk. 'As no policeman saw you, you are for once in luck, sir, and won't be fined for not obeying traffic signs.'

Ervinke's face fell.

'What do you mean, "no policeman saw you"?' he shouted. 'And if tomorrow someone kills me and no policeman is there to witness the crime, does my murderer go scotfree? A strange attitude, officer, I must say!'

The officer began to squint.

'Sir,' he said, 'now kindly leave me in peace, will you?'

'No, my friend!' Ervinke thumped the desk. 'We pay taxes so that the police will ensure public order! Or maybe,' he said with biting irony, 'my crime lapsed after half a day?'

'All right, sir!' the officer hissed and, crimson-faced, opened his big ledger. 'Give me all the details!'

'As you like,' thus Ervinke. 'So, as I said, I was driving down Shlomo Hamelech Street, at least I think so, I'm not quite sure. In any case I – '

'You parked near a bus stop?'

'I may have, it's quite possible that I parked, but only for a second, really . . .'

'You said you got out of the car!'

'I said I got out of the car? I may have said that I came back. Yes, I wanted – now I remember – I only wanted to see what had gone wrong with the engine. That's why I pulled up.

Am I to blame if something went wrong? Tell, me, am I to blame? Am I?'

'Sir,' the officer groaned, 'sir!'

'Listen.' Ervinke fell on the officer, whining. 'Couldn't you let me go just this once, really? From now on, I'll be more careful, so help me. It won't ever happen again, let me go just this once, please . . .'

'Sir,' the officer roared, 'get out of here!'

'Thank you, thank you!' Ervinke breathed and dragged me out into the street. In our wake, the desk officer collapsed in a limp bundle. One must do one's bit, mustn't one?

A proper exploitation of cheap manpower is one of the basic precepts of a healthy society. In simpler terms by all the known yardsticks, a slave society is tops. In our Near East this idea is not alien to the spirit of the local tribes, but we who aspire to be a bastion of enlightenment and progress in this neighbourhood cannot translate the idea into deeds, except on a strictly private basis.

Bailing Out a Friend

Last night, it will be remembered, the sluices of heaven opened, and the wells of the deep burst forth exactly under our little house in Afeka. As a result, at noon our overjoyed kids came to us and reported:

'Daddy, the basement wall is peeing.'

I rejected Rafi's ridiculous insinuation and would have forgotten all about it, except that our basement had in the meantime turned into a swimming pool. It transpired that without an early warning a mighty jet of water had shot out of the basement wall, enriching the local reservoir by at least a cubic yard every quarter of an hour. Moses must have felt like this when the water burst forth from the rock, except that his timing was better.

It goes without saying that we did not lose our heads.

'Water!' the wife screamed and ran out into the storm and hurried back in and ran out and screamed, 'Flood! Help! Police! Water! Good people! Basement! Fire brigade! Deluge! Municipality! Ben-Gurion! Help! Water!'

As for myself, I pounced on the phone and gaspingly alerted the legendary Stucks. Our plumber saw no reason for panic.

'No, it's not the plumbing,' he calmed me. 'It's only a lake under the house, it's a simple flood.'

'What should I do, Stucks, what should I do?'

'Soon it will be summer.'

'And in the meantime?'

'In the meantime better start bailing if you don't want the house to collapse over your heads.'

The wife tried to plug up the crack in the wall, first with plaster of Paris, then with plasticine and in the end with Band-Aids, which shows in what a state of nerves she was by then. Soon enough it became obvious that the only way to stem the virgin spring in the wall was to push your finger deep down the crack, thereby plugging it at least partially, and at the same time to grab two buckets and fill them with the bounty of the skies covering our chamber of horrors to a height of ten inches, and dash with them up the stairs and empty them in front of the house and go down and fill the buckets and run and plug up with your finger and dash up . . .

'Just imagine,' the little one consoled me, 'what they must have felt like in Florence when the whole city was flooded!'

In Florence they must have felt wonderful, I opined, because all that collapsed there was a few bloody statues and not my house. Apparently I was not born under the sign of the Water Bearer, because within half an hour the heavy water had brought me to the end of my tether. Amir also irritated me by launching paper sailboats and enjoying the whole show tremendously. Then at long last the Municipality sent the motor pump; they bailed out the water down to the last drop and left. Within a few minutes the basement had again filled up and I was again running up and down with the buckets, cursing the government and the whole rotten régime.

Then the telephone rang. Felix Selig could not have found a better time to announce his visit than in the middle of the flood.

'Felix,' I gagged, 'Felix, for goodness' sake . . .'

Whereupon the little one came skipping up the stairs and tore the receiver out of my hand:

'Yes, Felix, come,' she said, 'we'll have a nice cup of tea and a good chat. Come quickly.'

Not that the little one is smarter than me. She was just better rested, since she only had to plug up the hole with her finger, while I had to waste my strength bailing out our territorial waters. The Seligs arrived within half an hour, at the height of a cloudburst.

'You'd never believe what happened a few minutes ago,' the little one received them. 'Our basement suddenly became flooded. It's a real danger to life. Poor Ephraim is fighting the maelstrom singlehanded, nobody's helping him, he'll drown in the end. Please go home, we'll manage somehow . . .'

'What nonsense!' Felix flared up gallantly. 'We're staying!'

With that he took off his coat, rolled up his trousers and started running with the buckets, while his wife helped the little one with the plugging. This, gentlemen, I call international solidarity if you don't mind! Felix also proved himself a promising water carrier: because of his unflagging efforts the water stopped rising in the basement and after an hour or so stood hardly ankle-high. We simply didn't know how to thank these wonderful people who had such a well-developed sense of collective responsibility.

'It's so nice of you,' the wife whispered as she collapsed on a chair. 'What would we have done without you! Look, it's not worthwhile lugging up half-filled buckets, fill them up properly, will you!'

Felix's glassy stare intimated that at this stage he would not have minded distancing himself from us. His breath came in gasps and he staggered with the heavy buckets in his hands. The water had long ago passed ankle height and outside another downpour was raging obstinately. Luckily just then Zvika came in to ask whether we'd like to come to the second show. We found a big washbasin for him and arranged the three of them in a chain. As for myself, I limited my activities to technical advice and pace-keeping.

At 8.00 p.m. we were again alone with the flood. First the Seligs broke down, then Zvika collapsed on the stairs. Reluctantly we dismissed them and quickly ran down the list of our acquaintances who were in good physical shape. Because of the dangerous security situation, we could no longer rely on miracles.

'I think Weinreb plays tennis,' the wife remarked dreamily, 'and his wife is a big woman.'

The Weinrebs were somewhat surprised at the cordial invitation so late in the evening. Besides, they were meeting tonight a South American couple who had just arrived from Chile.

'Your friends are our friends,' the little one told them serenely. 'Our house is always open to them.'

So they came, all of them. Weinreb also brought along his table-tennis paddle, aiming to play a few sets down in the basement. And then, what surprise did fate have in store? By the time they arrived, water had burst into . . .

I felt completely exhausted, because every time the watches were relieved I had to shave and change into dry clothes so as to look more convincing to the newcomers. So what? Students from all over the world had come to Italy during this winter's floods, so no one will get hurt if we mobilize a few volunteers to help the victims of Greater Afeka's steep slopes.

'Hey hopp!' I clapped, keeping time for the rescuers. 'Hey hopp!'

The South Americans were particularly good. Their hourly output reached, by a cautious estimate, two cubic yards. Weinreb, as well, took the hard physical test rather well. The two teams succeeded in keeping abreast of the elements, and the water level in the basement dropped by a fraction of an inch, if not more. But then the wife committed a terrible tactical blunder.

'I'm sure you must be cursing us,' she said to the new team. 'Really, why should you kill yourselves because of our misfortune? In your place I'd go home, so help me.'

Why do women always have to talk? They went home. I find no words to describe our feelings. And as for our fair-weather friends: God forbid we should ever need them! By then we had become used to the hired-labour system and panic gripped us as we watched the water level rising steadily. I therefore rang up Meir Geiger because he lives on the other side of Afeka and could reach us quickly. Yona, Meir's wife, came to the phone.

'We'd come willingly,' she said, 'but our car's stuck in the mud.'

'So walk, it's only a few steps. And bring playing cards!'

'You know what, come and fetch us in your car!'

'Splendid! I'm coming!'

How pampered some people are! I left the little one to her plugging and sped in the darkness towards the Geigers'. I dashed into their house and tried at once to turn on my heel, but it was too late. Yona was standing in ambush behind the door.

'You'll never guess what's happened,' she whispered with quivering lips. 'A few minutes ago in our basement . . .'

I had fallen into their trap like a stupid kid. Clearly, this was why they had asked me to fetch them! Disgusting! I was so furious with the hypocrites that I spilled the water on purpose on the Persian rugs every time I came up with the three buckets. My head swam with annoyance and worry: here I was bailing out the Geigers' water with what little strength I had left, while my little wife was standing up to her knees in our private whirlpool, plugging up the hole.

'I phoned your wife,' Yona informed me. 'I told her how wonderful you are.'

'What?' I asked. 'What did she say?'

'She said that she's keeping her fingers crossed.'

In the end the Lord saved us, as always. The downpour decreased gradually and we sent forth a dove from us to see if the waters were abated from off the face of the ground, and the dove came in to us in the evening, and lo, in her mouth was an olive leaf: and we knew that the waters were abated from off the earth. And it came to pass in the nineteen hundred and sixty-seventh year, on the sixth day of the first month and seedtime and harvest, and cold and heat, and summer and winter, there came together the Weinrebs, the Geigers and Zvika and the couple from Chile and they nevermore spoke to us and it's a pity.

Ours is a democratic country par excellence, where the barriers between man and man have been pulled down long ago. We Israelis have become used to this horror, but tourists may expect some hardships.

A Holiday in Israel

'Waiter, please, waiter!'

'Yes, Mr Steinberg?'

'Breakfast for two.'

'Yes, sir, two breakfasts. Coming. I only wanted to ask you, Mr Steinberg, whether it's true that you are the writer I read about in the papers.'

'My name is John Steinbeck.'

'I see. Only yesterday I saw your photo in the paper, but there you had a bigger beard, I must say. They wrote that you are staying here a whole month and that you came incognito so that people should not bother you. Is that your wife?'

'Yes, this is Mrs Steinbeck.'

'She looks much younger than you.'

'I asked for breakfast.'

'Right away, Mr Steinbeck. All sorts of writers are coming to this hotel. Only last week we had the fellow who wrote *Exodus*. Did you read *Exodus*?'

'No.'

'I haven't read it either, such a thick book. But I saw *Zorba*. When did you write *Zorba*?'

'I didn't write *Zorba*.'

'Boy, did I enjoy that movie! I almost died laughing when that old broad started grinding her fat –'

'I want coffee, and tea for my wife.'

'So you didn't write *Zorba*?'

'I told you I didn't.'

'So why did they give you the Nobel Prize?'

'For *The Grapes of Wrath*.'

'So, coffee and tea, yes?'

'Yes.'

'How much do they pay for such a prize, Mr Steinberg? Is it true that they give a million dollars?'

'Couldn't we go on with this conversation after breakfast?'

'Sorry, but I won't have time afterwards. As a matter of fact, why did you come here, Mr Steinberg?'

'My name is Steinbeck.'

'You are not Jewish, are you?'

'No.'

'I thought so. American Jews don't tip. A pity you had to come just now when it's pouring. There's nothing to see. Or maybe you're looking for something special in Israel?'

'A soft-boiled egg, if you don't mind.'

'Three minutes?'

'Yes.'

'At once. I know that in America, Mr Steinberg, you are not used to talk so freely with waiters, but here in Israel we have atmosphere. By the way, I wasn't always a waiter. I studied orthopaedics for two years. But here you can't get anywhere without pull. The boss is from Poland —'

'Kindly order an egg for me.'

'Three minutes, Mr Steinberg. Listen, that was a movie, *Zorba*! Really, you laid it on thick! Our cook says that you are writing a lot of plays and movies, it's true, isn't it?'

'Yes.'

'What?'

'*East of Eden*, for instance.'

'I've seen it! So help me, I've seen it! Listen, I laughed! That scene when they tried to build a lift from the trees in the wood . . .'

'That's *Zorba*.'

'Right, that's *Zorba*. So of what do you write?'

'*Of Mice and Men*.'

'Mickey Mouse?'

'I'm starving, my friend!'

'Wait a minute. Mice, you said? Isn't that when that pretty actress tried to go to bed with that idiot?'

'I beg your pardon?'

'That one where there's such a big slob, that is, he is not so big at all, but they stuff pillows and things under his clothes and he looks big, so he comes with his pal who's thin but normal, and the big boy likes mice – '

'I know the contents of my plays.'

'Of course. So the big guy is huge and has to be watched all the time, that he shouldn't beat up people, but the son of the boss gets fresh with this actress, so he gets up and walks over to him quietly, and, boy – '

'Could I see the manager?'

'No need, Mr Steinberg, I'll fix you in a moment. I loved those mice, so help me! Did I laugh! But as for the end, excuse me, it's not good enough for you, Steinberg, it stinks, don't you agree? Why do you have to kill the big guy? Just because he's a little bit barmy? One doesn't kill off people for that, if you don't mind.'

'All right, I'll rewrite the play, but now bring me – '

'I'm ready to have another look at the play and tell you exactly what's wrong with it. I won't even ask any money for it. Maybe I'll visit you in America sometime. You know, I've lots to tell you privately, but not now. I'm too busy. So many things have happened to me, *Zorba* is nothing compared with – '

'Do I get that egg or don't I?'

'We don't serve eggs on the Sabbath. So, you hear, Mr Steinberg, if ever I'll tell you my life story, you'll make a fortune out of it, but I don't mind. I could write it myself, everybody's telling me, you're crazy you don't write a novel or an opera or something, but I'm so tired in the evening. I told them all to go to hell, I'll give it to Steinberg, I don't care.'

'Get off the table!'

'Two years ago, you hear, in summer, towards the end of summer, that is, I took the wife to Sdom, so about half-way there the taxi stops, the driver lifts the hood and pokes his head under it and you know what he said in the end?'

'Let go of my beard, will you!'

'No, he said: "Folks, the gasket's busted!" You hear, half-way to Sdom! I didn't make this one up, so help me! What did we do? We sat it out in the taxi all night. It was so cold, you just have no idea! But I leave it to you to make a best-seller out of it. It was a night, you hear, even your *Zorba*. ... Hey, where are you going? Mr Steinberg. I haven't finished. ... I've got fantastic stories to tell you. ... How much longer are you staying?'

'I'm flying back by the first plane.'

Every nation strives for what it hasn't got. The British are dying for sunshine, the Russians for dollars, the Israelis for antiques. Now, how the hell can a country which is still a minor have antiques?

The Geography of Antiquity

It all began with Hasya. Hasya is a friend of my wife's. She is also an antiques hound. One black day Hasya took the little one on a routine tour of the shops, and the wife came home ominously wild-eyed and kicked the magnificent Danish table in our living-room.

'Disgusting,' the little one remarked. 'Antique furniture's much prettier. From now on I'm going to buy only antique furniture. I'm going to devote my life to antique furniture.'

'Woman,' I said, 'what do we need furniture for? What do we lack in our apartment?'

'Atmosphere!'

Next day she went off with Hasya again and came back with one low chair which, instead of a seat, had an anti-seat of thin strips. This turned out to be 'an original piece of rustic,' as Hasya says, and a bargain. I asked the woman what it was for.

'For decoration. I'm going to make a toilet table out of it.'

She had bought the bargain at Wexler's. It seems there are only three expert antiquarians in the country altogether: Wexler, Yosef Azizao and young Bendori of Yaffo, who's also expert at restoring – i.e., he turns new furniture into old. These, the Great Three, rule with an iron hand over the twenty-eight items of antiquity in Israel that pass from hand to hand, from antique dealer to antique dealer, in unending circulation. Israel, you see, is the poorest country in the world as far as antiques are concerned. Neither the illegal immigrant ships nor the flying carpets carried Louis Quatorze cabinets aboard, not to mention Louis Seize. If a snip of Biedermeier or a chip of Baroque nevertheless does pop up here or there, all the professionals get to know about it at once, like the famous Florentine chiffonier at Kiryat Bialik . . .

'All my friends are dying to buy that chiffonier,' the little one told me, her eyes aglitter. 'They want no less than IL1,200 for it, but the dealers are still waiting for them to come down a bit.'

'And the friends?'

'They don't know the address.'

For that's the key to the whole industry: the address. If you have an address, you have an antique, you have all. Without an address you are nowhere. A true dealer, therefore, prefers to die under torture rather than let the least hint of an address escape his lips.

We shall, for instance, never know who it was who once upon a time owned the Neapolitan grandfather clock (1873) which shows the position of the moon as well. That is to say, for the past half-century it has been showing nothing but a moon eclipse because some of its cog-wheels have disintegrated and it isn't any use, except maybe as a toilet table. Anyway, the little one's friends are impressed by it, rather. Hasya considers that the gilded crystal eagle cage (1900) is awfully charming. Young Bendori, he who renews as well, rounded this bargain up for my wife. He got it from a new immigrant from Kenya, who had sold it to Azizao through Wexler. Yosef Azizao also got one leg of an original Windsor (1611), an impressive table leg, big, with a curly pattern creeping up it, a joy forever, heavy as hell.

'Woman,' I whispered after the porters had gone, 'what do we want this spare part for?'

'I haven't made up my mind yet.' She hoped, she said, that Azizao would find her some more legs like that one and when she had enough she'd put them together and have a table even, to make her toilet at. Facts are facts: our flat's now full of atmosphere from floor to ceiling. You can't take a step in any direction without tripping over Rococo relics. From time to time the telephone rings, I lift the receiver and the same is put down at the other end with not a word said. I know at once it's Wexler. Strangers walk around the flat putting on coats of varnish. Whenever the little one tosses in her bed at night I know she is dreaming about the Florentine chiffonier of Kiryat Bialik. 'I'm simply not table to forget that chiffonier,' she admits, and that was no printing error either.

All the same, the straw that broke my back was the Biedermeier cabinet.

By then I had already become rather allergic to the staircase. On this occasion the steps seemed extra loud, and the bed table coming in their wake was, indeed, something like a tombstone, weighing half a ton, give or take an ounce. They also brought, as an extra, the collapsible field bed of Field Marshal von Hindenburg (1918).

'I'm not a field marshal,' I roared. 'And why the hell did you buy that bed table?'

'To put next to my bed.'

'And what about *my* bed?'

She always buys singles. One chair, one candlestick, one bed table. As if we hadn't two beds and the collapsible Hindenburg.

'All right, all right,' the little one soothed me. 'I'll find you matching pieces.'

I went to see Wexler in the morning, my mind inexorably made up. I found the man in the middle of a process of interior undecoration: he was busy picking up antique items and throwing them pell-mell on top of one another, since – as I found out later – the greater the confusion in a true-blue antique shop, the more intense is the seek-and-you-will-find-a-bargain exhilaration experienced by the female buyers.

While Wexler was thus reorganizing I looked around. On one wall of his office hung a map of the country with about ten little coloured flags stuck in various places. The flags were inscribed: 'Renaissance footstool', 'Spanish Gobelin (1602)', and of course – near Haifa – 'The Florentine chiffonier'. North Tel Aviv had a black (!) flag reading: 'New site. Biedermeier cabinet. Louis XIII cage. Field bed'.

The blood froze in my veins: that was *us*!

I introduced myself, cautiously, as Zvi Weisberger. Wexler looked at me intently, turned a few leaves in a photograph album lying on his desk, then asked with a subtle smile:

'And how's the Windsor table leg today, sir?'

I blushed. 'The leg's doing fine.' There's no deceiving Wexler. Wexler knows all. Wexler has ways and means.

'How's the Missus?' he asked politely.

'The fact is,' I told him hoarsely, 'she'd better not know I've come here. Will she be here?'

Wexler stepped over to the teleprinter in the corner and read the message coming out of it: ' "Madame Récamier entered Azizao ten minutes ago. She's after a misericord. Over." '

'From there I suppose she'll go to Bendori because he has a misericord's address,' went Wexler's forecast, 'so we've got fifty minutes till she gets here. So what's it about?'

'Mr Wexler,' I said, 'I'm selling out!'

'Coffee?' asked Wexler, adding, 'Right, it's bad business to hold on to antiques for months on end. I hope you haven't told anybody else.'

'Just you. But bring your buyer when my wife isn't home, please.'

Wexler gave me a pitying smile.

'Take a buyer to an address?' he said. 'But that's suicide! Five years ago we once took some people blindfolded, so they took a good solid peek from under the handkerchief. Addresses aren't child's play. We shall transfer the commodities to our warehouse, sir.'

The red telephone on his desk started ringing. Wexler listened for a moment, then went over to the map and with slow deliberation struck the misericord flag at a point in North Tel Aviv. Madame Récamier had just bought it.

The organization of our project was exemplary.

Wexler called up young Bendori, he who renews as well, and informed him of the 'address liquidation'. Bendon turned him over to Azizao, who had just acquired a brand-new client in the form of a mad millionairess from South America. At 12.00 I took leave of my little woman, who was going on a routine tour in a state of unusual excitement, as if she were sensing something. And at 12.30 I opened the door wide for Wexler and the three deaf-and-dumb workmen, who took the whole antiquaboodle to young Bendori of Yaffo.

At 1.00 I was alone in the deserted flat. I stretched myself on the couch (1962) and burst out in merry song as if I had just been liberated from a submarine.

At 1.30 I suddenly heard those heavy steps outside. I rushed to the door in alarm. Yes. . . . Here they all were back again . . . the Rustic . . . the Windsor . . . the misericord . . . the whole zoo . . .

'Ephraim!' I heard the whoops of delight coming from the little one in the rear. 'I've bought some fantastic things! I've found the second cabinet!'

When she had entered the flat and discovered the single cabinet there, Madame Récamier burst into bitter sobs.

'You sneaks, all of you,' she wept. 'Azizao said the address was that of a mad millionaire from South America. All my savings gone! You doublefaced triplefaced . . .'

The blood rose to my head. I already knew that the selfsame antiques kept circulating among the selfsame buyers. But that my own wife would buy from her own husband's address . . .

I put an arm around the little one.

'Just because of what those hucksters did to us,' I hissed, 'we'll go out this minute and buy the Florentine chiffonier of Kiryat Bialik!'

How we got hold of the address, this is neither the time nor the place to reveal. It is a subject that will be discussed in antique circles for generations to come. Hasya told us that Wexler suspects that the little woman hid herself, one cool summer night, inside one of the Empire chests in his shop and from there overheard him discussing the chiffonier with his partner. Whatever the case may be, for a mere IL1,200 this proud piece of furniture is now doing its bit in the atmospheric household of yours truly, performing humble service, for the time being, as a toilet table. As of now we are the most renowned antiquarians in the whole region: all radar rays and teleprinters are turned on us. Azizao himself writhed in the dust at our feet yesterday, pleading with us to sell him something because ever since the blowing up of the address myth no antique dealer is able to justify his existence. I said to him:

'Yosef Azizao, the chiffonier stays!'

The Florentine marvel has completely upset the balance of power. It also satisfied a wee sadistic impulse: out of the twenty-eight antiques in the country, nine are in our possession! To a certain extent, our refusal to sell paralyses the entire market. Wexler and Azizao haven't recovered from the blow as yet. Only young Bendori of Yaffo manages somehow because he restores as well.

Countries which have no aristocracy create one.
Everything is relative: for an immigrant who came here in
1967, those who came in 1963 are aristocrats because they
have more seniority in pioneering. Now try to figure how
big is the gap if the difference is thirty-eight years, part of
them spent in the shadow of the gallows?

Lament for a Young Actor

PODMENITZKI: Hey, young man, step in here for a moment,
will you?

BEN TIROSH: Who, me?

PODMENITZKI: Yes, you!

BEN TIROSH: All right, Mr Podmenitzki. ... I've always
wanted to tell you, Mr Podmenitzki, that it is a great
honour for me to appear at rehearsals together with Mr
Podmenitzki.

PODMENITZKI: That's exactly what I want to talk to you
about, my boy. What's your name?

BEN TIROSH: Ben Tirosh. Joseph.

PODMENITZKI: How long have you been in the theatre,
my boy?

BEN TIROSH: Two months. Next week it's going to be two
months.

PODMENITZKI: They treat you right?

BEN TIROSH: I'm the happiest man on earth, Mr Podmenitzki. It has always been my dream to appear with great
actors of Mr Podmenitzki's calibre.

PODMENITZKI: Sit down!

BEN TIROSH: Thank you. Ever since I was a child I've been
crazy about Mr Podmenitzki. Ask my mother, if you like!
Now that we're going to appear in the same show, I'm so
excited at every rehearsal ...

PODMENITZKI: I can see that you are a smart boy, young
man.

BEN TIROSH: The name is Joseph Ben Tirosh.

PODMENITZKI: Yes, I hope we'll understand each other. Let's talk about the hanging scene. You are my executioner in the play if I'm not mistaken.

BEN TIROSH: It's a great honour.

PODMENITZKI: Don't interrupt me, young man. I like that scene and I like what you are doing at the rehearsal, at least as far as your acting is concerned. Until you open your mouth! When I get to the steps of the gallows, what do you tell me?

BEN TIROSH: Who, me?

PODMENITZKI: Yes, what do you tell me?

BEN TIROSH: My part?

PODMENITZKI: I want to hear it!

BEN TIROSH: 'Move,' I say, 'move.'

PODMENITZKI: Go on!

BEN TIROSH: 'Move ... you abomination ... you rotten dishrag ...'

PODMENITZKI: That's what you are telling me?

BEN TIROSH: Yes. That's my text.

PODMENITZKI: Rotten dishrag!

BEN TIROSH: Yes.

PODMENITZKI: How old are you, my boy?

BEN TIROSH: Twenty-two. I'll be twenty-two in July.

PODMENITZKI: Twenty-two! Very nice! And you're not ashamed to speak in such a tone to a veteran actor who has trod the boards of this stage for the past thirty-eight years?

BEN TIROSH: But that's ... that's my part. ... Mr Podmenitzki. It's all written down here ... and it also says that I've got to kick Mr Podmenitzki ... savagely ... in brackets.

PODMENITZKI: We'll come to that later!

BEN TIROSH: It's my part.

PODMENITZKI: Above your part you have a duty. Your duty is to learn! And to show respect towards the architects of the Hebrew theatre! What's your name?

BEN TIROSH: Ben Joseph. Tirosh.

PODMENITZKI: All right, my boy. So if you want to last

in the theatre, you better remember very carefully that Yarden Podmenitzki is a byword for the audience.

BEN TIROSH: For me, too, so help me.

PODMENITZKI: So why are you so happy and satisfied to curse and mishandle me, to humiliate me so utterly in this scene?

BEN TIROSH: I am happy? Where am I happy? I have to be happy, Mr Podmenitzki, because our director from France, Mr Monsieur Boulanger, explained to me . . . that I am content because I hate you – in the play, that is – because you are the head of the rebels whom we captured.

PODMENITZKI: For that goy I may be the head of the rebels. For you, my boy, I'm still Yarden Podmenitzki! How dare you kick me!

BEN TIROSH: I thought . . . I thought . . .

PODMENITZKI: The cheek! If the hangman had been played by Mischa Honigman, all right – a mediocre actor by any standard, but still, thirty years on the stage! But you, you snotty brat from drama kindergarten, you shamelessly curse your father for all the world to hear! What's the matter with you? Do you know what sort of parts I have played in my career? Heroes! Prophets! Kings! All right, so I am only the head of the rebels, I agree, fine, so is that a reason for spitting in my face on stage?

BEN TIROSH: Bou . . . Bou . . . Boulanger . . .

PODMENITZKI: Leave that fool alone. He hasn't got the faintest idea what theatre is! Anyway, he's going back to Paris. I'm staying here.

BEN TIROSH: Of course. I'm so sorry, Mr Podmenitzki. I'm still new on the professional stage.

PODMENITZKI: That's why I took the trouble of talking to you . . . what your name?

BEN TIROSH: Joseph Tirosh. Ben.

PODMENITZKI: Yes. So listen, my boy. As of tomorrow Yarden Podmenitzki does not drop on his knees before you on the stage. Is that clear?

BEN TIROSH: Absolutely. It's ridiculous, so help me, that you, Mr Podmenitzki, you . . .

PODMENITZKI: See? I'll stand erect on the stairs, and you'll say to me . . . what will you say to me?

BEN TIROSH: Move.

PODMENITZKI: Move, my foot! Tell that to your colleagues, the extras!

BEN TIROSH: Sorry. So maybe, 'Step up . . .'

PODMENITZKI: Step up, what?

BEN TIROSH: Sir! 'Kindly step up to the gallows, sir.'

PODMENITZKI: I've got a name, haven't I?

BEN TIROSH: Kindly step up to the gallows, Mr Podmenitzki.

PODMENITZKI: Stupid! My name in the play!

BEN TIROSH: Sorry, Step up, Mr Gonzalez!

PODMENITZKI: What Gonzalez? Frederico Albergo Marchio Amedeo Gonzalez!

BEN TIROSH: Yes, I'm writing it down.

PODMENITZKI: Write, write, my boy!

BEN TIROSH: Perhaps . . . perhaps I could drop on my knees before Mr Podmenitzki?

PODMENITZKI: An interesting idea, very interesting! It seems to me that you are blessed with a conceptual instinct, my boy.

BEN TIROSH: Joseph. Ben Tirosh. At your service.

PODMENITZKI: That's it, my boy. You won't have to change your part one bit. The inevitable is going to happen: as an executioner, you hate the guts of the rebel leader, but the moment you are faced with such a dramatic personality as mine, you become mesmerized. You come under the spell of the stage giant I am.

BEN TIROSH: Yes . . . Yes!

PODMENITZKI: And then I kick you from behind and say: 'Do your duty, you mangy dog!'

BEN TIROSH: I see. . . . Funny that I hadn't thought of this before, but what is Mr Boulanger going to say?

PODMENITZKI: He doesn't understand Hebrew.

BEN TIROSH: That's right. But after that . . . may I . . . hang Mr Podmenitzki?

PODMENITZKI: Don't bother. I'll hang myself.

BEN TIROSH: Thank you. So, as of tomorrow's rehearsal, okay?

PODMENITZKI: Okay, my boy. And there's no need to tell anyone about this. Let it be our little secret.

BEN TIROSH: Naturally, Mr Podmenitzki.

PODMENITZKI: Don't tell it to Boulanger, either.

BEN TIROSH: Of course not.

PODMENITZKI: May I trust you?

BEN TIROSH: One hundred per cent.

PODMENITZKI: Good boy! I can see a great future for you here, what's your name?

BEN TIROSH: Yossi.

PODMENITZKI: Yes. See you at rehearsal.

BEN TIROSH: Yes, dear Mr Podmenitzki, and thank you very much for everything! (*Walks home filled with a sense of professional achievement. At next day's rehearsal he is fired on the recommendation of Monsieur Boulanger.*)

CURTAIN

Podmenitzki will get rave notices from our most eminent
critics, thanks to the latest invention in Jewish stage
technique: remote-controlled criticism.

The Art of Getting a Rave Notice

'Look, the première ended only ten minutes ago, and there is
I. L. Kunstaetter running for the phone to dictate his review.
Again he'll be the only critic to make the morning papers.'

'Are you worried?'

'Not at all. He'll give us a fantastic review.'

'Are you sure?'

'One hundred per cent.'

'Is the show that good?'

'What show?'

'Your show, the show Kunstaetter is going to review.'

'What has the show got to do with the review?'

'I thought that . . . after all . . .'

'Don't be ridiculous. The times are long past when a theatre
manager like myself could rely on the excellence of his production. Nowadays, in the age of guided criticism, it's only
ice-cold reasoning that counts.'

'For instance?'

'For instance, the choice of a play. Why do you think I
chose a Polish drama from the thirteenth century?'

'Because Kunstaetter . . .?'

'Right. Because Kunstaetter is Chairman of the
Israel–Poland Friendship Council.'

'I see. That should rate you a special review.'

'Not necessarily. Now and again he has to prove to his
readers that, though he is Chairman of the Council, he is quite
objective towards Polish art, and then he is ruthless.'

'So why aren't you worried now?'

'Because I did not trust to blind luck. I waited patiently until two months ago, when Kunstaetter tore to shreds the Polish dance group which visited the country, and then I said to the boys: "Now we can come out with a Polish play without any danger from him."'

'That sounds easy.'

'It only sounds so. Nowadays a good review depends on thousands of small details. After all, Kunstaetter could conceivably praise the play to the skies and yet completely demolish the production.'

'So what could you do against that?'

'I apply the well-tested roulette system. I watch out for a succession of five blacks, then bet on red – and get away with the show. See?'

'No.'

'See this little notebook? Here I write down whatever Kunstaetter said about other premières during the last few months. Here: on May 23, 1967 – "a minor horror"; on June 7, 1967 – "a slapdash job"; on June 19, 1967 – "how much longer?"; on June 30, 1967 – "obnoxious clowning"; on July 6, 1967 – "a miserable farce". Five times black; now; according to the laws of roulette, for the sixth time he is bound to write a good review, otherwise they'd suspect him of bitterness. I expect to get at least "plastic, highly expressive acting, creating good rapport with the audience" out of him.'

'Quite a job.'

'We have ordered a small computer for next season, but for the time being I have to handle things by myself. In any case, the direction and décor will earn Kunstaetter's fullest praise.'

'How do you know?'

'We are linked to Plotkin.'

'Come again?'

'I always try to come out right after Gershon Plotkin's première at the Chamber Theatre. Now, everybody knows that Kunstaetter hates Plotkin like the pest because Plotkin once said that he was dumpy. Ever since, Kunstaetter automatically slaughters Plotkin's directing. That's only natural. However, Kunstaetter knows that while Plotkin is used to the harsh words about his directing, he will absolutely blow his top if, in the same paper, side-by-side with his being slaughtered, he'll read kudos for the director of another show running at the same time. So I always come out with our new productions close on the heels of Plotkin. That ensures unreserved superlatives for our directors. As a rule, whenever Kunstaetter is complimenting someone, he's trying to annoy someone else.'

'You said the décor will also get praise?'

'Yes. Here we deal from a position of strength. Six weeks ago, at the unveiling of the memorial, the father of our stage designer, himself a well-known sculptor, boxed Kunstaetter's ears because of some sort of art review. The incident was widely reported in the press and now Kunstaetter has no alternative but to praise the daughter's work, otherwise people will say he's just being spiteful.'

'What a lucky break that her father should have beaten him up just at the right time!'

'Luck doesn't come into this at all. He did it on my instructions. "You want your daughter to get good reviews?" I asked him. "Then bash in Kunstaetter's head." Believe me, it's not at all easy to coordinate all these factors. Take the casting, for instance. I gave the lead to an actor who is mediocre, Yarden Podmenitzki, and thereby had the benefit of a doubt.'

'What's that?'

'The publisher who publishes Kunstaetter's collected reviews year after year is also named Podmenitzki.'

'I see: he is the actor's kin.'

'Not at all. But Kunstaetter is under the impression that he is. After all, it's a rather uncommon name. So Podmenitzki always steals the show with him. Here, see what my notebook says: April 3, '65 – "I was surprised by Podmenitzki's refreshing playing"; August 11, '66 – "The surprise of the evening was . . ."; February 27, '67 – "To our pleasant surprise, Podmenitzki." Before this première, just to play it safe, I sent Podmenitzki to ambush Kunstaetter in front of the publisher's office. They bumped into each other on the staircase, the actor going up, the critic coming down, and by a cautious estimate this should guarantee Podmenitzki a "subtle, well-balanced and amazing performance".'

'I can see you've been thinking of everybody.'

'Not of everybody. That would be a fatal mistake. You always have to leave a weak link in the chain on which the critic can vent his ire. If you don't plan for that in advance, he could hurt something really valuable. So better hand him his victim on a platter. In our show, for instance, the lightning rod is the composer of the music.'

'How does that work, if I may ask?'

'Very simple: I looked for a composer of Hungarian origin. As you know, Kunstaetter is allergic to Hungarians, for hereditary reasons. So the music of our composer will be "anaemic, raucous and utterly alien to the spirit of our country!" The poor guy will absorb the whole quantity of unavoidable bile.'

'My hat is off to you, sir.'

'I haven't finished yet. You have to think of the smallest details. The show was ready to go way back in June, but I held up the première until the humidity had dropped somewhat, because it has a marked influence on him. Above 85 per cent he is merciless, that's a well-known fact. Everything is under control. I also surrounded his seat with a steel ring of actors' relations, and to tickle him pink even before the curtain rose, I seated his keenest competitor, the critic S. Greenbotater, three rows behind him, right on the aisle.'

'Just a second. So what's Greenbotater going to write?'

'Don't be funny, he translated the play.'

'Perfect planning, I must say.'

'It has to be perfect. More than sixty theatre people work months on end on such a play, so I can't take chances when so much is at stake. Every show deserves professional defence, and certainly so does a beauty like ours. Are you going to see it?'

'I think I will.'

'When?'

'I don't know yet. I'm waiting to see the reviews.'

Tortures which the strongest man cannot endure are nowadays no longer the exclusive province of the secret police. They are now within easy grasp of the man in the street. All you need to practise them is a locked room, a bed, matches, a few garments, nylon stockings, various handbags, and your wife.

They Arrived Tomorrow

'Ephraim,' the wife shouted from the other room. 'I'm almost ready.'

The time was 9.30 p.m., the date December 31. The wife had been sitting in front of the wardrobe since sundown, preparing herself for the part at Tibi's in honour of the Gregorian New Year. I reminded her that we had promised our hosts to be there at ten o'clock, whereupon the little one said that it was quite all right to be fifteen minutes late, since at first the party would in any case be boring as there would as yet be no atmosphere.

'All my dresses are old rags,' the little one remarked, wearing a toga. 'I haven't got a thing to wear.'

I hear this remark every time we leave the house for any reason whatsoever, as if her wardrobe were not bursting with clothes. The idea behind the remark is to make me doubt my adequacy as a provider and in general to give me a nice inferiority complex. In fact, I don't understand a thing about her dresses, in my view they are all awful, and yet I always have to choose which dress she'll wear. Why?

'I've got that plain black dress,' the little one ticked off the alternatives, 'or the blue one with the high slit.'

'That's it,' I said, 'the one with the slit.'

'It's too solemn. How about the chemise?'

'Yes,' I said. 'That sounds good.'

'But isn't it too sporty?'

'Sporty?' I scoffed. 'What do you mean sporty?'

What, in fact, is a chemise? Only God knows. I closed her zipper and went to the bathroom for a shave while the wife changed her stockings for a more suitable colour. After much searching, she found a proper stocking, but it had no mate. This is an elementary law: Suitable stockings are always lonely in life. So now she had to take off her chemise and look for another rag better suited to the pearls she got for her last birthday from her husband's wife.

'It's ten,' I alerted her while hurriedly dressing. 'We'll be late!'

'Never mind,' thus she. 'So you'll hear two off-colour jokes less.'

I was already in my festive trousers, but the wife was still puzzling over the question: pearls or silver brooch? The pearls are more decorative, but the brooch is more impressive. It would be a miracle if we made it by eleven. I started reading the daily press. The wife was looking for a belt to go with the silver brooch and was absolutely dejected: she had no suitable handbag to go with the new lacquered belt. I started writing a few letters, short stories, essays ...

'I'm ready,' the wife shouted from the other room. 'Come and close the zipper.'

I wonder what would honest women do about their zippers if their husbands escaped in good time? My guess is they wouldn't go to New Year parties. Nor are we going. The little one ties a small nylon apron around her neck and makes up her face. She applies the foundation that goes under the powder. The eyes are not yet touched up with mascara, they are still looking for shoes to go with the bag. The light pair happens to be at the shoemaker's, the black ones with the high heels are beautiful but you can't walk in them, in the low-heeled ones you can walk but they are low-heeled ...

'It's eleven!' I got up, fuming. 'If you don't finish in a minute, I'll go by myself!'

'I'm ready,' the wife calls from the other room. 'You can't do the hully-gully anyway.'

She takes off the little nylon apron because she has decided after all to wear the plain black dress. Why complicate things, right? But where are the stockings to go with it? Where are the dark stockings? Eleven thirty. I decide on a clever trick: I get up, walk with heavy steps to the entrance, shout a furious Shalom, bang the door (as if I had left) – and hold my breath as I hug the hall wall . . .

Silence.

She has broken down apparently, the little one. A strong arm always helps. How did old man Nietzsche put it: 'When going to a woman, don't forget the whip.'

Five minutes go by in utter silence. It's a little uncomfortable to spend the rest of one's days in a dark hall. Perhaps something terrible has happened in that room . . .

'Ephraim,' the wife shouts, 'come and do up my zipper!'

She has again slipped on the chemise (the plain black one has a burst sleeve seam). She has changed her stockings as well and is in a quandary over the pearls.

'Give me a hand, for goodness' sake,' she says. 'What do you suggest?'

I suggest we go to bed and have a good night's rest. Without another word I change into pyjamas.

'Don't be ridiculous.' The little one is furious. 'I'll be ready in ten minutes.'

It's midnight. All over the country, chiming clocks are ushering in the new year. Good night. I turn off the little bedside lamp and fall asleep. The last sight I remember was the wife bending down in front of the mirror, the nylon apron around her neck, tracing her eyebrows. I hate that little apron the way no little apron was ever hated. If I even think of it, my hand clenches in an iron fist. In my dream I was the late Charles Laughton, who as Henry VIII, it will be remembered, chopped off the heads of his six wives. Horrible mass scenes haunted my dreams. Women were carted off to the gallows while the crowds cheered. They changed stockings in the tumbril, smeared green paint around their eyes and one of them shampooed her hair and applied henna . . .

After a deep and refreshing slumber of an hour and something I woke up next year. The wife was sitting in front of the mirror in the blue dress with the high slit, and was still painting her eyebrows with a black pencil, the tip of which she had burned with a match. A terrible weakness took hold of me.

'You know, old boy,' my id whispered inside me in a completely indifferent voice, 'you married a mad-woman.'

I looked at the watch: one fifteen. Id is right, this little woman is kookie. Suddenly the horrible thought flashed through my mind that I was in hell. As in Sartre's *No Exit*, the severest punishment of the sinner is to be locked in a small room with a woman who keeps dressing-dressing-dressing . . . forever!

As a matter of fact, I was a little afraid of her. Just then, she was moving all her little things from her big black handbag into the small black handbag. She was almost dressed — wait! — except for her hairdo. The big question was: to cover the forehead or leave it exposed? A few strands of hair which make all the difference in the world.

'I'm ready,' she announces, 'get up!'

'Do you think it is still worthwhile going?'

'What do you mean, is it worthwhile going? Then why did I have to hurry. Don't worry, there'll be enough of those disgusting cocktail sausages left.'

She was a little angry at me, I could feel it, because of my unconcealed impatience. The little apron was lying on the floor next to her. Quietly, I stretched out a foot, pulled it over with my toes and disappeared with it into the kitchen. I burned that apron with my own hands. I placed it in the sink and put a match to it, then watched the flames the way the Emperor Nero did in his time. It left an unpleasant smell, but I really had no choice. As I returned to the room, the little one was standing in front of the mirror in a quasi-finished state. I closed the zipper of the plain black dress and started dressing myself, hardly able to keep my eyes open, when — poof!

The ladder!

As I watched her from behind, I discovered . . . a ladder . . . in her left stocking . . . terrible! As the old Sanskrit proverb says: 'Whoever changes stockings changes everything.' Good Lord, let her not discover the ladder, let her discover it only at the party if at all . . . after all, it's way back, the ladder . . . make a miracle, Almighty . . .

I went quietly to my study and sat down at the desk.

'Don't waste time now,' the wife shouted from the other room. 'What are you doing there?'

'I am writing a scenario.'

'I'm almost ready!'

'I know.'

The work progressed nicely. I sketched in broad strokes the character of a great artist – a painter, violinist, humorist, what have you – who was expecting a great deal from life, but somehow got bogged down and was marking time, year after year. Why? Because of a woman, folks, who kept holding him back all the time. The writing proceeded with amazing ease. The artist realized his desperate plight and made up his mind to leave the woman who hampered him so grievously. On that long sleepless night he made a fateful decision. 'Boy,' he says to himself, 'you'll get up and get the hell out of here.'

Heavens!

The wife is in the bathroom washing her face. Two a.m. It's two o'clock. She finds the colour of her eye-lashes vulgar and puts on new makeup. For that you have to wash the face, service and grease it, the works. Everything from scratch. Utter despair grips me. Everything in the room seems to be mocking me. There is little sense in such a life. I walk over to the cupboard, take out a strong necktie and knot it to the top of the window. Let's finish and be done with it . . .

The wife somehow senses that I am standing on a chair.

'Stop it, will you,' she says, 'and close my zipper, please. So what are you beefing about now?'

What am I beefing about? Good Lord, do I know what I'm beefing about at 2.30 in the morning, dressed in a shirt with a starched front and a dark jacket and striped pyjama pants, while my little wife with one hand applies spray to her hair and with the other gropes in the cupboard for gloves? Gloves? It's hard to believe, but it looks as if this time she has really made it. A ray of hope stabs through the dismal darkness. So it has been worthwhile holding out. She is actually ready. In a little while we will go out and have a good time. Bursting with energy, the little one moves her little things from her small black handbag into her big black handbag and removes the pearls. I pull my dark trousers over the pyjama pants. Everything is a little hazy. Outside dawn is breaking. Somewhere in Nazareth the church bells are ringing three a.m. in honour of the new Gregorian year. My nose is somewhat red because of the suppressed sobs. The little one remarks that I ought to perk up and, besides, I am stubble-faced – what, haven't I shaved?

'I did shave,' I whisper, 'long ago when you started dressing, I did shave.' I go into the bathroom and with a trembling hand remove the three-o'clock shadow. I have lost my youth during this night. The face of a tortured old man is looking out at me from the mirror, the face of a man whom life has passed by. The face of a husband.

'I must always wait for you,' the wife is carping in the other room. In the meantime she is looking for a suitable hat, because one of her locks is not sitting right. A last look in the mirror, a last dab at her face, a light brush of the powder which keeps falling . . . everything is fine . . . perhaps a little liquor is still left at Tibi's . . . are we going? Yes, let's . . .

The door opens. Impossible! We're off. We are off to the party.

'Wait!' The wife stops, thunderstruck. 'There's a ladder in my left stocking!'

The rest is lost in the cosmic darkness from which there is no escape. The big zipper closed in on me. Inside the ghostly infinite, at a distance of millions of light years, there is music at the party – the party we never made.

Ever since Creation, which, according to the Jewish calendar, took place on October 5, man has been striving to immortalize his name. To do this he is ready to burn down the Temple of Diana at Ephesus, or to sire sons. World Jewry has the benefit of an additional alternative: its brethren in the State of Israel are ready to inscribe any public building in their name. All they have to do is to erect the building. The following story deals with a small fry in this racket.

Housewarming

Ervinke was in a dither, as well he might be.

For the first time since his establishment, my friend had moved into a spanking new apartment on Salamander Street, Holon. It was indeed a solemn occasion. The contractor cut the blue-and-white ribbon in the staircase with beaming officials from the Municipality looking on, while one of the neighbours played Sousa marches on an accordion and the seventy-eight donors from abroad started streaming towards the entrance.

A woman in a wide-brimmed straw hat stopped on the doorstep and her eyes lovingly caressed the sign fixed on the jamb: *This wooden door was donated by Mrs Matilda R. Weinreb, Boston, Mass.* Next to her a pleasant tourist couple were polishing the brass plate over the doorknob which read: *This doorknob is the donation of the S. T. Englander family (San Francisco, Calif.), to mark the birth of their second grandchild, Gloria Veronica, sister of Sylvia Anne Mary, may they both live and prosper!*

Ervinke passed a tray of sandwiches among the donors, stopping from time to time to empty a glass with his benefactors. He was moved almost to tears, as I have already mentioned.

'Without them I would never have been able to put a roof over my head,' he whispered to me on one of his rounds. 'It's really touching. They hardly know me. My only link with them is that mimeographed letter.'

It was indeed a simple but highly effective letter Ervinke had in its time dispatched overseas: 'Dear Brother/Sister in the Diaspora: Progress in telecommunications and the consolidation of democracy the world over have made it possible even for the man in the street to claim the inalienable right of every good Jew to immortalize his name in Israel through a one time, limited generosity, a natural right which until now was enjoyed only by those wealthy enough to endow palaces, yeshivot and assorted museums. I am therefore happy to inform you that registration has started for the revolutionary instant endowment scheme called "Small Donation – Big Sign" which rewards even small-scale generosity with nice, big signs . . .'

Ervinke related: 'The response was beyond my wildest hopes, so that I had to screen the candidates most carefully.'

A noisy argument could suddenly be heard coming from Sunshine Hall – i.e., the bathroom. A tourist, beet-red in the face, was pointing at a metal plate bearing the inscription: *This bathroom would never have been covered with ceramic tiles but for the generosity of James B. Sunshine of Buffalo, N.Y.*

'This is disgraceful,' Mr Sunshine roared. 'The contract clearly stipulates "an impressive gratitude plate made of pure brass, size 14×10.5 inches, placed in the centre of a conspicuous location, well lighted.'

Ervinke was visibly embarrassed. The mini-donor's ire was obviously justified: his sign was completely dwarfed by the huge marble slab fixed above the sink. *Let this back-brush carry the names of Mr and Mrs M. K. Bialazurkevitz, Chicago, Ill.*

'There's just so much room on the walls,' Ervinke apologized. 'After all, there are seventy-eight signs in this flat, including the big charter signs.'

Just then the large Philadelphia group which came within the Charter Agreement climbed up to the roof for photos. Its spiritual leader, Rabbi H. P. Todot, was leaning with understandable pride against the gold-plated emblem glittering in the rays of the sun: *This antenna rises on this roof thanks to the inhabitants of the City of Brotherly Love, Mr and Mrs S. S. Wagnerman, Miss Emily Z. Krupskind, the I. T. Seligson family, Mr P. U. Firelady, Jr, and his children John, Franklin, Evelyn, Harry, Gusti, William and Daisy May.*

Gradually the sandwiches ran out, the accordionist left for reserve duty, the ceremony drew to a close. Ervinke tied on a bow tie, then launched into his housewarming speech in which he expressed his deep-felt gratitude to all those who had come from overseas at their own expense, just to be present at the inauguration of the apartment with its flatware.

'I could kiss them all,' Ervinke said to me, 'all! Except that one there – Blumenthal!'

I followed my irate friend's glance. In a corner of the flat I saw a stocky tourist, his eyes brimming over with tears, his hands shaking as he rubbed and polished a bronze plate, attached to nothing, on which was engraved in huge letters:

This bronze plate was donated by N. B. Blumenthal, Bronx, N.Y., in the year 1967.

In a country which won its independence only a few years ago, you can still climb the ladder of command several rungs at a time. Naturally, this does not mean that the man at the top has to change. On the contrary, as a rule he stays the same hail-fellow-well-met Jew who is always happy to meet his old pals. The question is only: for what time does the Secretariat fix the appointment?

The Kiss of Rokotowsky

The festivities marking the sixteenth birthday of Sichin village some time ago were followed with great interest by the whole country, so much so that the then Prime Minister, Mr David Ben-Gurion, promised to grace the veteran settlement with his presence. The Old Man's participation was officially confirmed by the Prime Minister's Office, the necessary preparations for the important event were undertaken, and everything seemed to be going swimmingly until Rokotowsky got into the act, as the idiom goes.

Indeed, the trouble started on the day veteran member Munik Rokotowsky, one of the village's founding members, informed his friends that he intended to realize his dream of a lifetime and kiss the Prime Minister the moment he met him at the festivities.

'I'll give David such a smacking kiss,' Rokotowsky said, with an impish grin, 'that he'll jump sky-high with joy.'

As we said, Rokotowsky was a veteran member of the village, and his place was certainly in the forefront of the celebrants, but such irresponsible talk created a certain amount of uneasiness among the organizers of the festivities. They therefore invited the old fellow to appear before the committee.

'Comrade Rokotowsky,' they asked him officially, 'is there any truth in the rumour that you are planning to kiss the P.M. and Defence Minister?'

'And how!' Rokotowsky smiled blandly. 'The moment I

catch sight of David, I'll plant a huge kiss on his face, so help me!'

'Comrade Rokotowsky,' they said to him, 'are you sure that the P.M. and Defence Minister will like that?'

'Now, what a silly question is that, really!' Rokotowsky sounded offended. 'After all, we worked together in an orange grove fifty years ago. My hut was the third to the left of his hut. David will jump with joy, mark my words, he'll simply jump.'

The delicate question was brought up at the next meeting of the Sichin village council. The debate was rather heated. One of the comrades, by the name of Yasha Guberov, accused the council heads of taking advantage of the festivities for strengthening their positions and creating nepotism.

'If Rokotowsky kisses him,' Guberov threatened, 'I'll kiss him as well!'

'Comrades! Comrades!' The chairman pounded the table with his fist in an attempt to bring order into the pandemonium which had broken out. 'We can't have everybody doing just as he pleases! Let's vote!'

Munik Rokotowsky – as could be expected – obtained a majority of four votes and was appointed, now at public request, official kisser on behalf of the village. But in order to avoid any unpleasantness at the time of implementation, the village secretariat sent a registered letter to the Prime Minister's Office, couched in the following language:

Dear Comrades,
We take pleasure in notifying you that one of our members, Munik Rokotowsky, has informed us of his intention to kiss the P.M. and Defence Minister when he visits us during the festivities of our village. After a short debate, the council agreed in principle to Comrade Rokotowsky's plan, but we naturally warned him that final permission was subject to agreement by the P.M.'s Office. We therefore request you to inform us of your attitude and give us the necessary technical instructions.

In the hope that this request by a veteran village and party member will meet your agreement, we are yours in comradeship,
Sichin Village Council

A fortnight later a letter arrived from the P.M.'s Office, and in it the okay for Comrade Rokotowsky's kiss. 'Though,' it said in the letter, 'the P.M. does not remember the above comrade except in a very hazy way, in view of the festive atmosphere and the emotional circumstances we are not opposed, in principle.' The letter emphasized that the kiss would have to be given in a cultured and dignified way – that is, after the P.M. got out of his car and advanced towards the local council building, Comrade Rokotowsky would be allowed to break out of the ranks of the cheering populace and press a kiss on the P.M. and Defence Minister's cheek, at the same time holding him in a comradely hug, which should under no circumstances last more than thirty seconds. For reasons of security, the council was also requested to forward at their earliest convenience to the Prime Minister's Office four passport photos of Comrade Rokotowsky and his identity-card number.

The letter caused great satisfaction among the inhabitants of Sichin village, as now a more personal character would be given to the forthcoming festivities. The only disgruntled person was no other than the father of the idea.

'What do you mean, half a minute?' The veteran villager fumed, deeply hurt. 'Who does he take me for, a soft-boiled egg? And what if David doesn't let go of me and keeps hugging me again and again?'

'These are official arrangements,' they explained to him. 'They are based on extensive public experience, every detail is carefully thought out. Times have changed, comrade. We are living in a modern state, not in the Turkish era.'

'All right,' Rokotowsky said, 'then I won't.'

'What won't you?'

'I won't kiss David. We worked in the same grove, my hut was the third on the left of his, maybe the second. If I can't hug an old pal the way I want, then I won't do it at all.'

He was an obstinate fellow, Comrade Rokotowsky. Perhaps that was why he was still a simple villager after all those years. The council's efforts to make him change his mind were in vain.

'Then why did we take out the permit for you?' they stormed at the oldster. 'What will it look like if the P.M.

comes, gets out of his car, waits to be kissed and there is no one around to do it?'

What's even more embarrassing, the organizers had already leaked something to the press, hinting that 'at the opening of the Sichin village festivities, one could expect a spontaneous meeting between the P.M. and one of the veterans of the village, a meeting which promises to be most emotional.'

And now – what a disgrace!

'Kiss him, Munik, kiss him,' they implored the rebel, 'otherwise we'll send someone else in your place, so help us!'

'Send someone else!'

Munik Rokotowsky locked himself in his home and sulked while the council convoked an emergency meeting at which some extremely heated words were exchanged. Comrade Yasha Guberov requested for himself the privilege of the jubilee kiss, claiming that to all practical purposes he was next in line after Rokotowsky, but the council chairman proposed a democratic casting of lots, while others proposed to call in somebody from outside more experienced in these matters. In the end it was decided to appeal to the Prime Minister's Office for a decision on the personnel reshuffle.

'Dear Comrades,' thus the message of the council, 'for technical reasons beyond our control, we had to dispense with Comrade Rokotowsky's services as P.M. kisser during the visit. However, since feverish preparations for the intimate event have been all but completed and everybody is keenly looking forward to it, we should be very grateful if you could assist us in choosing a new candidate among the villagers. The candidate of your choice would naturally also act in line with the directives previously laid down.'

About a week later, there arrived a young man of severe mien, the official representative of the Prime Minister's Office. He surveyed the field and carried out a quiet selection among the villagers – i.e., he struck from the list of the would-be kissers those of above average height, as well as all moustache wearers. In the end he chose a pleasant-looking villager who happened also to be the head of the local party chapter. Afterwards a precise course was drawn on the village map, with a broken line marking the direction from which the lucky headman was supposed to break through the cordon. To be on the safe side, clear markings were drawn on the piazza in front of the council building: the hugging spot was enclosed in a whitewashed circle, while the take-off point was designated by an X.

Several rehearsals on the day preceding the opening of the festivities sufficed to ensure a smooth performance. The lucky party boss received a detailed briefing regarding the intensity of the hug, in consideration of the P.M. and Defence Minister's age, while the problem of timing was solved in the most efficient way, it being agreed that the kisser himself would count slowly to thirty and then would let go. The representative of the Prime Minister's Office gave proof of great skill in these arrangements, handled the police angle as well, and even remembered to have the sun at the photographer's back during the meeting.

'The P.M. and his entourage will arrive at 11.20,' the representative concluded. 'At exactly 1200 hours they will leave this place. I hope everything will go off right.'

And indeed, due to the meticulous planning, the ceremony went off flawlessly. The P.M. and his entourage arrived at 11.20. On their way to the council building, the lucky party boss broke through to the Old Man, fell on his neck and kissed him. The P.M. smiled cordially, though he was somewhat disturbed by the fact that his assailant muttered 28–29–30–*break!* After the kiss the Old Man continued towards the little girl with a bouquet of flowers in an atmosphere of heartiest fellowship and informality, which was also reflected in the loud cheering.

Only one villager took no part in the general rejoicing. Munik Rokotowsky stood all by himself at the tail end of the line of celebrants, tears streaming from his eyes. They had worked the groves together, this was *his* kiss. The kiss he would now never place.

A Scandinavian crown prince once remarked: 'To eat or not to eat', and ever since, mankind has been beating out its brains over the question: to have a little something before you go to the Pomeranzes' or to put your trust in the big meal – hopefully – waiting there?

Peanuts for the Masses

'Ephraim, are you sure it's for dinner?'

'I think I'm sure.'

I had explained to the wife a hundred times if I had explained to her once what the situation was, and yet she kept on asking. I had spoken on the phone to Mrs Pomeranz and accepted with thanks her invitation for Wednesday, at 8.30 p.m. And ever since then we'd been endlessly analysing that conversation, because Mrs Pomeranz hadn't said it was for dinner, on the other hand she hadn't said it wasn't.

'You don't invite people for 8.30 sharp without dinner.' This was the wife's view. 'Apparently it's dinner.'

I thought so, too. If they don't intend to feed you, they say 'don't come before eight' or else 'between eight and nine' but never 8.30 sharp. Besides, I thought that Mrs Pomeranz had particularly stressed the hour. She had said at 8.30, stressing the 'at', and besides, there had been a definitely dinnerish tone in her voice.

'No, it's for dinner, I'm almost sure.'

I proposed to call Mrs Pomeranz and as if by the way ask her if she was preparing something, but the wife said that wouldn't be nice. Anyway, on that Wednesday we were busy all day and just had sandwiches for lunch, so that by nightfall we were quite hungry, but the wife said it was not worth while eating anything at home.

'I know the Pomeranzes,' thus the wife. 'If it's for dinner, we're going to get the works.'

Before our mind's eye there appeared a tea trolley groaning with shishkebab, turkey, salads, chips, and savories tastefully arranged. If only they wouldn't talk a lot, at least until after dinner.

We arrived at the Pomeranzes' and right away started worrying. First of all, no one else had arrived yet, and even the Pomeranzes were still dressing. Our concerned glances swept over the salon and there was not a hint of anything solid. The equipment was standard: chairs and armchairs around a low table, and on the low table a big plate of peanuts, almonds and raisins, a few olives and pieces of white cheese with plastic toothpicks sticking out of them, a cucumber, salt sticks. It flashed through my mind that maybe Mrs Pomeranz had after all said on the phone 8.45 and not 8.30, or maybe she had not mentioned the time at all and we had only discussed Fellini's $8\frac{1}{2}$.

'What would you like to drink?'

Mr Pomeranz came in, still tying his tie, and poured us a John Collins. This is a lovely drink, a third brandy, a third soda and a little Collins, we were always glad to drink it, but this time we were completely turkey-orientated and craving massive things. We felt a terrible emptiness in our stomachs while we clinked glasses, smiling cordially.

'Lechaim,' Pomeranz said, and added, 'What do you think of Sartre?'

I took a fistful of peanuts and tried to analyse existentialism as it affected us, but only too soon it transpired that I hadn't enough material. After all, what are a plateful of peanuts and a few almonds for a grown man? The wife was sitting under the same constellation. She had finished off the black olives at one stroke and had played havoc with the white cheese. When we came to the bombing of North Vietnam, all that was left on the low table was a few lonely pieces of cucumber.

'Sorry.' Mrs Pomeranz smiled, with raised eyebrows. 'I'll get some more.

She took the devastated plates to the kitchen. As she opened the door, we tried to catch a glimpse of the kitchen, hoping against hope that some unusual preparations were going on there, but the results were literally frightening. The kitchen looked completely sterile, the atmosphere alarmingly calm. In the meantime several more guests had arrived – at 9.15 (?) – and my stomach suddenly let out such a fearful screech of anguish that I almost died of shame. The conversation somehow turned on the Old Man's successful trips overseas.

'You can say what you like,' somebody said, 'nothing hurts Ben-Gurion.'

Nothing? I would have liked to see the Old Man if they had fed him for a whole day on peanuts in America! I, for instance, felt slightly sick after the second plate. Not that I had anything against peanuts – quite the contrary. Peanuts are very nutritious food with a lot of proteins, only they can't serve as ersatz for turkey, bread and fish salad with mayonnaise.

I looked up. The little woman, chalk-white, was gripping her throat; it was obvious that the cucumbers and the raisins were fighting the John Collins inside her. I threw myself on a fresh cargo of white cheese and I think I also swallowed a toothpick. I simply couldn't stop. Mrs Pomeranz looked at us askance, then exchanged a few words with her husband and returned to the kitchen to replenish her stocks.

'Nu,' someone remarked at my elbow, 'the number of unemployed is growing day by day.'

'Of course,' I answered, 'the government is starving us.'

I could hardly speak because of the salt sticks in my mouth. As a matter of fact, why did I have to listen to this crap about unemployment when here in the middle of the salon a whole family was dying for a piece of bread? The little wife finished off the third lot of peanuts, and the first traces of panic appeared on the faces of our hosts. Pomeranz took out of a cupboard some toffees, which quickly joined the rest of the victuals. Remember, we had had hardly a thing since the morning. The salt sticks were setting up such a racket in my mouth that they deafened me from inside. The skin was drum-tight on my belly and I felt slightly dizzy. By cautious estimate, I had swallowed about four pounds of peanuts, several tins of sticks and a sea of salt. I had long ago lost any trace of self-control. I kept hiccupping and groaning and had all sorts of psychedelic visions. The little woman had turned into a chunk of toffee and her eyes were imploring mutely. Mr Pomeranz brought some olives from the neighbours'. I had reached a stage where the very thought of peanuts caused me unspeakable nausea. Only let's not think of food. Let's not think of any food at all.

'Ladies and gentlemen, please come in!'

Pomeranz opened the door of the next room and before our eyes there appeared a big table with a snow-white cover ... plates ... glasses. ... Good Lord ...

Mrs Pomeranz rolled in a tea trolley loaded with turkey, mushroom soup, chips, asparagus, salads ...

'Please be seated.'

The rest I don't remember.

'A stiff-necked people' – that is what the Almighty called us, hinting that we are as stubborn as mules. For five thousand years they wanted us to give up our faith and we did not oblige. For two thousand years they tried to make us settle down elsewhere and here we are back in Jerusalem. Now they want us to give up smoking.

How to Break the Habit

'Pardon me, sir, have you got a cigarette?'

'Sorry. I've stopped smoking. I read those shocking reports in the papers.'

'So have I, but I got over them.'

'How did you manage?'

'It's all a question of willpower. At first I thought I would go out of my mind. After all, it's rather nasty to read day after day that you are headed for lung cancer and stomach aches and haemoglobin and all that. On the day the *Jerusalem Post* carried the report of the U.S. Health Agency on the dangers of excessive smoking, I was seized by panic and there and then made up my mind to stop reading newspapers.'

'Good idea!'

'Wait! I held out for a whole week – not even the headlines, nothing! But in the middle of the second week I felt that unless I read a paper right away, I'd go stark, raving mad. After all, you can't cut yourself off from the world completely, can you? One evening I broke down, went over to the neighbours' and begged them to lend me yesterday's paper. I devoured it. The first newspaper in more than a week!'

'I can imagine.'

'Wait! I turned to the inner pages and the first thing my eyes fell on was the report of the British Ministry of Health. It knocked me flat. They said that every man who smokes more than thirty cigarettes a day was bound to lose his masculinity, or something. I smoke two packs a day.'

'Hmmm . . .'

'I realized that I had to do something drastic, otherwise I'd sink deeper and deeper into this nightmare. "To stop reading newspapers entirely won't do," I said to myself. "I'll have to break away from the reports gradually!" With that, the struggle started. On the first day of the cure I still found it necessary to burn the paper so as not to break my oath and read about the hazards of smoking. But after a few days it became easier, I read the news carefully and tried just to skip through the inside pages. But one night while reading a magazine in bed the vice again gripped me: my eyes fell on the mortality chart drafted by the Weizmann Institute. It was a terrific temptation, sir! I was dying to read! I bit my lips to shreds, pushed a pillow into my mouth, but I did not read a word of the report!'

'I envy you, so help me!'

'It was tough, but now I'm all right. Nowadays, if I see a report in the paper, believe me, I simply ignore it. I'm rid altogether of newspaper reports. And ever since, I feel wonderful, as if I had been reborn.'

According both to real-life experience and to statistics, the average Israeli simply adores lawsuits, regardless of whether he is the plaintiff, defendant, or lawyer for the defence. A fight is a fight, isn't it? The only thing of which we are in mortal terror is to be summoned to court as witnesses. Because a defendant may still win an acquittal – the witness never.

See No Evil! A Sequel to Kafka's *The Trial*

Friends and acquaintances may have noticed that lately I have been conspicuous by my absence. The truth is that I got involved in a lawsuit concerning a certain fatal traffic accident, in consequence of which I doubt that I shall ever again be able to show my face before honest and law-abiding folk.

The traffic accident I got involved in happened on the Tel Giborim Highway. More specifically, on my way home one bright noon I saw a huge government limousine collide with a bicycle rider and reduce him to a heap of bones. The limousine had jumped a red light and was speeding the wrong way on a one-way road. Besides, the driver was clearly drunk. Being the only witness on the spot, I agreed to the policeman's request that I show up in court and tell the whole truth and nothing but.

The courtroom was packed with a motley crowd drawn by the information that the limousine had been driven by a personality much in the public eye lately. The personality also had the benefit of a large independent income and had secured the services of a top lawyer, who had thoroughly prepared his brief, as I was to find out soon.

Since I was the only eyewitness, the trial started with my interrogation. After my personal data were taken, I was handed over to the defence lawyer, who rose and informed the court of his intention to prove that I was an irresponsible person, a congenital liar and a hardened criminal whose testimony was not worth the paper it was written on. According to the procedure of cross-examination, the lawyer posed questions which I did my best to answer.

DEFENCE: Mr K., is it true that in 1951 you were wanted by Interpol for armed robbery and perjury?

I: That's not true.

DEFENCE: You mean to say that it is not for armed robbery and perjury that Interpol wanted you?

I: I was not wanted at all. Why should I all of a sudden be wanted by Interpol?

DEFENCE: So by what police force were you wanted?

I: I was not wanted by any police force.

DEFENCE: Why weren't you wanted?

I: I know why not?

Yes, that was a fatal mistake. I ought to have answered: 'I was not wanted by any police force in the world because I have never in my life broken the law.' However, I was terribly tense, probably because of the large crowd and the relays of photographers who had taken potshots at me all the way to court, while during my testimony reporters kept sprinting to the phone booths informing their newsrooms on how my testimony proceeded. The lawyer from time to time exchanged a few words with the defendant and continued the cross-examination:

DEFENCE: Is it true, Mr K., that you were sentenced to a year and eight months in prison for committing an indecent act on a minor?

I: That's not true.

DEFENCE: So what sentence did you draw for committing an indecent act on a minor?

I: I did not draw any sentence for committing an indecent act on a minor.

DEFENCE: So on what charge were you sentenced?

I: On no charge.

DEFENCE: Do you mean to say, Mr K., that in our country people are sentenced to jail without a charge sheet?

I: I was never in jail.

DEFENCE: I didn't say you were in jail, I said you were sentenced to jail. Cheap tricks won't help you, Mr K., just answer yes or no!

I: I was not sentenced to jail, and I did not do time.

DEFENCE: Then what was the sentence for your indecent act on a minor?

I: There was no sentence of any kind.

DEFENCE: Why not?

I: What do you mean, why not? Because there was never such a trial.

DEFENCE: Then what sort of trial was there?

I: I know what sort of trial?

He had trapped me again. While prepared to testify on the Tel Giborim traffic accident, I was not at all ready for such autobiographical questions. Besides, I was greatly depressed by the hostile attitude of the audience. They kept whispering among themselves and pointing me out to one another; some grinned sarcastically, and what's more, during the fifth hour of my interrogation a news vendor did a brisk business in court hawking the special edition of an enterprising newspaper whose main headline screamed the whole width of the front page: K. COMMITTED INDECENT ACT ON MINOR! Under this, in much smaller type, it read: *K. Denies – His Interrogation Continues.*

My knees started knocking when I saw the headline, and the thought of my poor wife caused me great anxiety. She is a rather simple woman who does not know exactly what 'Defence' means, and could well think that the court itself had levelled these grave accusations at me, though they are of course quite untrue. In any case, I had to go on absorbing the heavy punishment of the cross-examination, as prescribed by court procedure.

DEFENCE: Is it true, Mr K., that your first wife divorced you after you escaped for the second time from the lunatic asylum, and asked the police to make you return her jewellery which you had pawned?

Here the court ruled that I would not have to answer questions relating to my marital status. I pondered the judge's words and came to the conclusion that it would indeed be a shame to mix up my wife in this sordid affair, especially as we had never separated and loved each other dearly. But my silence only increased the public's animosity and a fat lady in the first row even spat at me in disgust. All the same, I held fast and refused to answer the lawyer's next question: whether it was true that I had deserted from the army in '48. Further, whether it was true that I used to chain my son to the bedpost.

Here – when the chains were mentioned – a regrettable incident occurred which greatly detracted from the dignity of the proceedings: namely, a garage hand among the spectators rose to his feet cursing and tried to throw himself at me and break my skull with a thick iron rod, but the judge ordered the cops to expel him from the hall.

All this hardly served to improve my position, and seeing in the lawyer's hands the list of additional questions on my imaginary crimes, I became hysterical and started shouting at the top of my voice that I wanted to confess my guilt, that I and only I had run over the cyclist on the Tel Giborim Highway.

His Honour drew my attention to the fact that, for the time being at least, I was only a witness, and the interrogation continued.

DEFENCE: Is it true that as recompense for similar testimony over a 'fatal' traffic accident, you received in December of last year three valuable Persian rugs from one of the country's wealthiest importers?

I: That's not true.

DEFENCE: Do you mean to say, Mr K., that you have no rugs at home?

I: I have some.

DEFENCE: Are they of local or foreign manufacture?

I: Foreign.

DEFENCE: Thank you. I have no more questions!

The defence rested its case and the lawyer smugly sat down amid the acclaim of the public.

By this time the paper had brought out a second edition featuring my photo and the following headline:

CARPET SCANDAL UNROLLED IN COURT
K: I GOT RUGS, BUT NOT FROM THE EXPORTER!
DEFENCE: 'LIAR! LUNATIC!'

I asked permission to go home, but it seems that the prosecutor, too, wanted to ask me about the accident. He asked me whether in my opinion the defendant had driven recklessly. I answered in the affirmative and was dismissed.

The court usher smuggled me out through a back entrance to avoid the lynch mob which had assembled in front of the building, armed with clubs and stones, soon after the third edition.

Since then I have been lying low, as I pointed out at the beginning of the story, waiting for the years to pass and the defence lawyer's questions to be forgotten.

A typical Jewish characteristic is the desire to save mankind, if necessary against its will. One of the most outstanding representatives of this attitude is good old Karl Marx, who invented classless society, equality and production without exploitation. So far, all that mankind has achieved along these lines is a few kibbutzim in Upper Galilee.

The Angry Old Man

On the way to Haifa we dropped in at a Tnuva restaurant for a snack, and our eyes fell on an elderly Jew in khaki shorts, his face framed by a huge, scraggly beard. He was sitting at one of the tables, eating salad and a dish of yoghurt. His broad face looked strangely familiar.

I walked up to him. 'Pardon me, haven't we met somewhere?'

'Could be, I'm at all the ideological seminars,' the elderly Jew answered. 'The name is Marx, Karl.'

'Good Lord, not the father of Marxism?'

The old man's face lighted up.

'Yes.' He blushed with pleasure. 'I thought they had all forgotten me.'

'Forgotten?' I exclaimed. 'Workers of the World Unite?'

'I beg your pardon?'

'I mean. . . . Workers . . . of the . . . World . . .'

'Oh, I see.' The old man furrowed his brow, trying to remember. 'There was something of the sort, wasn't there? Went down quite well with the masses. Long ago, though. Take a seat.'

I sat down next to Marx. Only a few years ago, back in the old country, I had studied him thoroughly. I was especially good at 'cycles of economic crises' and at 'the rottenness of the imperialists'. It was nice to meet him in person. Though, frankly, he looked rather decrepit – at least 130 years old, a pitiable sight. I tried to raise his spirits a little.

'Only last week,' I said, 'I saw your photo in the newsreel.'

'Yeah, so I was told. In China, what?'

'Yes. In the May Day parade half a million people carried your picture and that of Mao Tse-tung.'

'Ah, Mao is a nice kid.' The old man smacked his lips as he took small spoonfuls of yoghurt. 'A few weeks ago he sent me his picture.'

The patriarch carefully unwrapped the genially smiling Mao's miniature portrait and showed it to me. Across a corner of the photo the Chinese leader had scrawled his dedication: *Tse meine rebbe un groissen Lehrer, haver Karl Marx, mit groiss Achting, Mao.*

'A pity I don't understand Chinese,' Marx said and returned the photo to his pocket. 'They are all right. They do marvellous things. But the others . . .'

'The Russians, you mean?'

'Don't even mention them to me! I had such great expectations of them! "Pioneers of World Revolution", or whatever they called themselves. Today they have a party line with the Yanks. A little while longer, and there won't be any difference between the two.'

'But, Master,' I pointed out, 'you yourself wrote in the *Manifesto* that the aim was a society without national friction.'

'I?' The old man sucked his teeth. 'Did I write that?'

'Yes, yes. That was the ultimate aim, you said.'

'Ah, the ultimate aim! But they are just at the beginning, don't you see? First of all you have to bring down fire and blood on the capitalists.'

'And what about peaceful coexistence?'

'There is no such thing! I never wrote anything about any coexistence. That's an invention of those crooks in the Kremlin. Do they want to beat the capitalists by producing more TV sets? Mao is right: those "nouveaux riches" no longer have an inkling of what Marxism is.'

'And the Marx-Lenin Institute in Moscow?'

'A hoax! They teach poems about the beauty of Mother Russia. I understand that one of the students asked what will eventually bring down the capitalist system. You know what the instructor told him? Income tax!'

'He's got something there.'

'And the class struggle? And the dictatorship of the proletariat? Why did they have to throw those overboard? There is not a trace of it left there, sir. Marx-Lenin Institute indeed! If you must know it, I prefer Marks and Spencer in London. They at least know what capital means.'

I tried to calm him. 'Take it easy, Mr Marx. Things may yet turn out all right.'

'Only the Chinese!' the old man fumed. 'Only they! They'll teach you a little communism, you bastards! They'll teach you to suffer! Don't worry, they'll make such proletarians out of you that your own mothers won't recognize you. Seven hundred million Chinese, "gute Marxisten alle, bis zum letzten Mann", do you realize what that means?'

'But they need more time.'

'They have plenty! You just wait! I knew what I meant when I wrote in *Dialectical Materialism*: "In evolution, quantity influences ideological quality and quality ... again ... engenders ... historical quantity. ..." Though I never quite understood that passage. But the Chinese have got the atom bomb, haven't they?'

The old man finished his frugal meal, wiped his plate with a piece of bread and rose to go.

'Got to return to the chicken coop,' he said. 'I work as a hired hand in the kibbutz across the road. That's all that is left to me in the whole world: the Chinese and you. "A git yontef" ...'

While the British are giving up their cherished uniqueness with a heavy heart and are changing over to the decimetre and right-side driving, our country's rock-firm resistance to the temptations of New Year's Eve is wavering. But we still celebrate the Happy New Year on October 5, because on that day the World was created, it will be remembered. And to strengthen our case we swamp each other with greeting cards on the eve of the one and only true New Year.

A Card from Moshe

My attitude towards New Year greeting cards has been positive all along. Ever since my arrival in this country I have gone into the card-sending business with a will, honouring the people I most loved at the time, such as my landlord, the collector of income tax, the man in charge of 'constructive loans', theatre critics, bank directors, heads of housing departments, and a host of other people I felt an inner urge to greet on New Year's Day.

In exchange, those lean years brought me cards from the postman, the grocer, the furniture store and the corner laundry, as well as from incipient actors, dentists, an interior decorator and Moshe Sharett, then our Foreign Minister.

There hardly ever was a reply to the cards I sent out, or if there was, it came with a great delay. I, on the other hand, would always answer promptly, using the same-size card and the same script. What particularly touched me was the thoughtfulness of Moshe Sharett, whose best wishes always arrived about ten days before the holiday. It goes without saying that I was flattered, though surprised. The Foreign Minister was considered one of our outstanding personalities, and it was characteristic of the man's modesty that he signed himself simply, 'Your friend Moshe Sharett', with no addition of pompous titles or official insignia. Many was the time I discussed with my wife Sharett's demonstrative interest in my fate, and we agreed that here was a born linguist-etymologist and lover of literature who had discovered in my column startling language innovations which had prompted his noble gesture. Naturally, I always reciprocated with a warmly worded and grateful card, which I dropped into the mailbox with my own hand, thus stressing the importance I attached to it.

For months, with calculated nonchalance, Mr Sharett's card would be left lying on my desk and my visitors would cast jaundiced glances at it.

Then the heady pioneering period came to an end and was followed by a more sober era. With an inner shudder I realized that when I sent out greeting cards I did it with the ulterior motive of gaining money and influence. This realization was bad enough, but even worse was the discovery that the cards did not advance my chances in any way, but were simply water down the drain. I therefore gradually slowed down the flow of greetings to a trickle, and people also ceased sending me their good wishes. Apparently I no longer had a constant following – except for Mr Sharett. Because our relationship had transcended by far the commonplaceness of holiday cheer. Here was an example of mutual esteem between two intellectuals of calibre who hardly knew each other personally, being engaged in different fields of endeavour: one an elder statesman, the other a promising satirical writer. Yet, once a year each of them pulled out his pen and saluted the other as if he were saying: 'I am full of esteem for you, sir, and your work, may you persevere in it for many, many years. God bless you.' It was beautiful. It was heart-warming. To my credit be it said that I never tried to take advantage of New Year cards. Though I made a point of being present at most of Mr Sharett's banquets and lectures, I always contented myself with a light wave of the hand and a shy but somewhat conspiratorial smile. He also behaved with noble restraint towards me. There definitely was rapport between the two of us.

On the eve of New Year's Day I would come home and ask my wife: 'Has Moshe written?' and he had.

With his characteristic thoroughness he would not forget me even while he was abroad, and the customary modest card would arrive in due course, covered with his neat writing:

'Your friend Moshe Sharett.' Small wonder if my replies became warmer and more intimate as the years passed. Once, if memory serves me, I sent a valuable oil painting to Mr Sharett in Singapore, where he had gone on a Socialist mission. My message went as follows: 'Full of gratitude and admiration, I wish you, dear Mr Sharett, a happy and prosperous New Year. Your protégé who draws encouragement and inspiration from your annual tokens of friendship. May you live to 120.'

And then the Polish circus came to town.

I am rather fond of this sort of popular entertainment, especially if they send me complimentary tickets for the gala opening. I enjoyed the show very much, especially the lions, and said so to an acquaintance of mine who happened to be the public-relations man of the circus.

'A marvellous show.' I shook his hand. 'My compliments to the artists.'

'Thank you very much,' the man replied. 'This is quite a compliment coming from you, who are famous for your reluctance to reciprocate.'

'Exactly what do you mean by that?'

'Look,' he said with the publicity man's long-suffering smile on his face. 'I obstinately send you New Year greeting cards year after year, and you have never bothered to drop me as much as a line, or even to say thanks over the phone. But never mind, I'm sure you have more important people to think of.'

'But that's ridiculous,' I snorted. 'I answer every single greeting card, including yours! I even remember the address. Moshe . . . Moshe . . .'

'Sharett,' the man prompted me, 'Moshe Sharett, 4 Horseshift Street.'

As an outcome of this painful experience, will readers kindly take note of the following: from now on, no replies will be forthcoming to New Year greeting cards which do not clearly indicate the profession and exact address of the legibly spelled well-wisher.

Complex-ridden psychiatrists claim that Jewish parents pamper their children inordinately because they want to give them everything they themselves missed in life. Maybe there is something in this. This writer, for instance, never tasted the intoxicating flavour of striped chewing gum in his dismal childhood, and today he would be ready to go to the end of the world to get some for his kids. Or anyway he is ready to go abroad for a while. Sans kids, naturally.

Les Parents Terribles

The decision once taken, we proceeded to plan our holiday abroad with single-minded determination. One problem is still vexing us: what are the children going to say? Rafi, of course, is already a big boy, one can talk to him as sensibly as to an adult. He understands that Mom and Dad were invited by the King of Switzerland and one cannot say no to a king, because he would be furious. So much for Rafi, but what to say to Amir, who is only two-and-a-half: that is, in just the period when the child is most closely attached to his parents?

A very difficult problem indeed. We know of cases where irresponsible parents left their baby for a fortnight and as a result the child picked up all sorts of complexes and later on failed dismally in geography. A little girl in Netanya, we were told, whose monstrous parents went to Yugoslavia for a month, began showing symptoms of paranoia, is lean as a stick and left-handed.

We discussed the problem at lunch with the wife. But hardly had the first French sentences left our mouths when sadness that beggars description spread over the child's face. He looked at us out of his big eyes and asked in a weak voice: 'Why? Why?'

Clearly the child was sensing something, the child was upset. He is very attached to us, little Amir is. We exchanged glances, the wife and I, and there and then dropped the idea of travelling. Foreign lands are twelve to a dozen, but sons a man has only two, one of them still an infant. We won't travel and that's that. Do we have to travel? How are we going to enjoy Paris with the thought persistently buzzing in our head that back home Amir may by now be writing with his left hand? Kids are not a pleasure cruise, sir, but a vocation in life, and if you are unable to make sacrifices for your kids, forget about them and travel abroad.

This was exactly our case. We wanted to travel abroad quite particularly. It would be a real hardship to renounce. We wanted to travel abroad.

But what to do with big-eyed Amir?

We consulted our downstairs neighbour, Mrs Gov Arie, whose husband is an airline pilot, so that she gets free tickets twice a year. It appeared that she breaks the news to her children gradually. She describes to her offspring the beauty of the scenery over which their parents will fly; what's more, they take photographs of those wonderful places and bring the pictures home. Thus the child partakes of the parents' pleasure, feels as if he himself had been on that trip. A bit of tact, a little understanding, that's all. Just a hundred years ago, had Mrs Gov Arie's children been told that their parents had flown to America, they would have had hysterics, or at least become compulsive pickpockets, but nowadays, with the advent of psychoanalysis and the aeroplane they bow gracefully to the inevitable.

So I settled down to a man-to-man talk with Amir (his Mom was also present).

'You know, Amirele,' I said to him, 'there are such high mountains in – '

'Don't go!' Amir shrieked. 'Don't go! Amir not alone! Amir, Daddy, Mom! No mountains. Don't go. Don't go!'

Tears streaming from his blue eyes, he pressed against us, trembling in every limb.

'We won't go!' I yelled in unison with my wife. All the scenery in Italy is not worth a single sparkling tear in the eye of our darling! A smile of his is dearer to us than all the world's blooming sunsets. We'll stay home, finished. When the child grows up, turns sixteen or twenty, we'll see. Staying home won't kill us.

Thus the problem would have found its happy solution, but

for a further complication. That is, next day we decided to go after all. We love Amir insanely, but we also love to travel abroad, that's a fact. So what to do with the brat?

We did some serious thinking. An acquaintance of ours is a so-called infant-psychologist. We called on her and described to her our delicate situation in all its details.

'You made a serious blunder,' the psych chided us. 'The child cannot stand lies, his soul is still unspoiled. "Tell me the truth!" he says, so you have to speak to him honestly, openly. For instance, you ought not to pack your luggage in secret, but, quite on the contrary, in his full sight, so that he should not believe that you are planning to run away from him.'

At home we took down the two valises and summoned the child to our room.

'Amir,' I said to him straight from the shoulder, honestly, without beating about the bush, 'Mom and Dad – '

'Don't go!' Amir yelled. 'Don't go! Amir loves Mom and Dad! Amir not alone! Don't go.'

He was all atremble, the child. His eyes were swimming in tears, his nose had reddened, his arms were flailing the air in mute terror. Something could happen to him, God forbid! We hugged him to our breasts: 'We won't go! Who said we are going? We took down the valises because we are looking for toys to give Amir! Mom and Dad are staying home forever, only here, always, only Amir, all the time Amir, who needs Europe?'

But clearly this time the shock has been too violent: the child is disconsolate and holds to my trousers with an iron grip. His whole heart is in his desperate sobs, the Weltschmerz of generations. We are on the verge of tears ourselves: have we committed an irreparable blunder? Have the wellsprings of his tender little soul been damaged, Heaven forbid?

'Why are you standing around like a fool?' the little woman shrieks at me. 'Fetch him some chewing gum!'

Amir's sobs are cut off so suddenly one can almost hear the screech of brakes.

'Chewing gum?' he asks. 'Dad brings Amir chewing gum from 'broad?'

'Yes,' I reply very quickly, 'with stripes!'

The child gets up, the child does not cry, the child is completely relaxed.

'Chewing gum with stripes! Striped chewing gum!' Amirele hop-skips around the room, clapping his little hands. 'Go, Daddy, go now 'broad! Bring Amir lots of chewing gum.'

Eyes shining, face composed, he is the prototype of the happy child.

'Go!' Amirele yells. 'Go quickly! Go abroad! Why don't you go? Why?'

See, now he again cries. His big blue eyes are streaming tears, his whole body is trembling. He drags the heavy valises over to us.

'Soon we'll go,' we promise, 'soon!'

'No! Now!'

So that's why we had to advance our departure by a whole week. The last days were especially difficult because of the pressure the child applied on us to leave at once. Even at night he woke us to ask why we were still here. He is very attached to us, the kid. We'll bring him lots of striped chewing gum. We'll also bring some to the psychologist.

To prosper, industry needs an ample supply of organized, industrious and steadfast workers, a vast reservoir of skill and know-how. Of the above qualities, the 'organization' angle is all right. Ours is a country of powerful trade unions. In line with this, every Hebrew industrialist knows that it is his duty to supply his workers at least once every two months with a reasonable pretext for striking. If he fails to cooperate in this field – strike!

I'm All Right, Moishe!

Though Israel Corks Ltd was founded only a few years ago, it quickly became one of the most flourishing enterprises of our growing economy. It satisfied not only almost all the local demand for well-turned high-quality corks, but even expanded into the Cyprus market and captured it. True, the plant enjoyed particularly sympathetic treatment at the hands of the authorities – that is, it received a 165 per cent subsidy on each export dollar, but there was nothing wrong with that, seeing that the raw material, high-grade oak cork, had to be brought in through Switzerland, and the workers through the Labour Federation. Economic circles considered Israel Corks Ltd one of the country's most profitable companies, whose income would really start spiralling upward after our happily joining that unspeakable European Common Market.

The beginning of the labour crises can actually be pinpointed: September 27.

On that day Mr Steiner, founder of the company and chairman of its board of directors, called in the head of the workers' council, one Joseph Ginzburg, and told him:

'The plant is left all night long without supervision. It's a real wonder no one has burgled it and carted everything away. This does not actually concern you, Ginzburg, but for the sake of good order I herewith inform you that the management has decided to hire a night watchman.'

'But that definitely does concern me, Steiner,' Joseph Ginzburg answered. 'The workers' council has to approve the decision.'

'I don't need any approval from you, Ginzburg,' Mr Steiner replied, 'but all right.'

As a matter of fact, the argument turned out to have been quite superfluous. The workers' council unanimously approved moving an elderly workman called Trebitch into the night-watchman position on condition he be given certain benefits, such as a night allowance in view of the loneliness he was going to experience, and naturally a third of his salary income tax-free, never mind what they write in the books. The management accepted the conditions without protest and old Trebitch started his night beat. For a while all was smooth sailing, but after the first night's watch Trebitch went to his councilman and told him:

'Ginzburg, I'm afraid all by myself.'

The councilman informed the managament of this new development. Mr Steiner again gave proof of his anti-labour attitude and demanded that the old coward be returned to his former job.

Joseph Ginzburg cut the furious director down to size. 'A human being is not a cork that you can toss about, Steiner,' he told him. 'We've already put a new worker into Trebitch's old job and we certainly won't let him be fired because of your lack of social feeling. For the sake of good labour relations I propose to put on a second watchman with the old man.'

Steiner surrendered, as production costs for each two-centimetre cork ran to only twelve agorot and he was loath to interfere with the joy of production within the plant. On that night, therefore, two watchmen were sitting in the cramped room in which the actual cork production took place. But next morning old Trebitch walked up to Joseph Ginzburg and told him:

'It's better now, Ginzburg, but we get terribly hungry at night. We need a buffet.'

The clash between Mr Steiner and the councilman this time took on epic proportions. The management would perhaps have agreed to hiring a woman to make hot soup for the two watchmen, but it rejected out of hand Ginzburg's demand that an electrician be employed to turn on the lights in the evening and turn them off at the crack of dawn.

'What next?' Mr Steiner shouted. 'Can't they turn off those lights themselves?'

'First of all, don't shout, Steiner, because I'm not impressed,' Ginzburg remarked with his characteristic calm. 'Secondly, of course they can handle the electricity – after all, they are not children, are they? However! However, turning off lights is certainly an additional duty which could take away another man's job. If the management wants to have the two watchmen do forced watches during the night, the council has no objections, but a watchman does not have to work as an electrician as well!'

Mr Steiner blanched.

'Ginzburg,' he whispered hoarsely, 'that's exclusively the management's business!'

'Steiner,' thus the councilman, 'let's ask the arbitration board.'

As usual, they took out the collective contract and quoted sub-paragraph 27: '. . . the management may act independently regarding all technical arrangements within the plant, provided this does not change working conditions.'

'Here you are,' Joseph Ginzburg pointed out. 'It changes them!'

'It does not change them!'

'It does!'

The argument raged for thirty-six hours before the Secretary of the local Workers' Council intervened and proposed a compromise which was also a face-saving device for the management of Israel Corks Ltd. It was agreed on principle that a woman would be hired to run the night buffet and a qualified electrician to handle the lighting; in fact, however, it would not be he who would turn the lights on and off, but the woman. The electrician would only supervise her from a technical point of view.

'It is my sincere hope,' the Secretary declared at the signing of the minutes, 'that this will end all misunderstanding in this important production branch, and that now all constructive forces will be devoted exclusively to the implementation of the new economic policy, the increase of production, the freezing of wages – '

'That will do,' Ginzburg interrupted him. 'No need to go into details.'

Two whole days passed at the plant in an atmosphere of quiet with no disturbances.

But on that Tuesday Mr Steiner called in Councilman Ginzburg. The Chairman of the Board was sitting in his big armchair waving a sheet of paper in his hand.

'What's this?' Mr Steiner hissed. 'What on earth is this again?'

'An ultimatum,' Ginzburg answered. 'Why?'

The document in Mr Steiner's shaking hand was a summary of the demands of the four night workers, who had elected the veteran watchman Trebitch as their leader. It boiled down to the following points: (a) hiring a qualified porter to open and close the door for the night shift; (b) raising that part of the salary of which the income-tax authorities are ignorant, never mind the book juggling, by 15 per cent, in view of the dry winter; (c) a young watchdog; (d) pensions; (e) an adequate number of mattresses and blankets.

The authors of the ultimatum called their demands a 'minimum programme' and hinted at severe disciplinary steps to be taken unless immediate negotiations were opened for the settlement of all differences.

'Ginzburg,' Mr Steiner gasped, his face livid, 'I'll close down this damned factory, so help me!'

'That would be a lockout not approved by the Labour Federation and might prove rather dear,' the councilman sneered, and added: 'Who are you anyway, Steiner, to threaten us all the time?'

'I'm the owner of this firm! I'm its founder! I'm its director!'

'Look, I'm in no mood for your jokes, Steiner. The plant belongs to those who work in it.'

'Who works here anyway? Making a cork costs us fifty-five agorot.'

J.G. walked up and down for a while in a pensive mood, then drew up in front of the director.

'Steiner,' he said sadly, 'you are fired. Get your salary for last month and beat it.'

A keen disappointment was in store for Joseph Ginzburg. The Union of Cork Workers within the Labour Federation did not approve of the dismissal.

'Comrade Ginzburg,' they told the councilman at an informal meeting, 'you can't fire a boss with fifteen years' seniority in the trade without paying him severance pay. Couldn't you give in on a few points in the ultimatum? For instance, why do you need a young watchdog?'

'You are lackeys of capitalism,' Ginzburg dryly replied. 'You are traitors to the working class and you are selling us down the river. But just think of the next elections, comrades!'

And he banged the door furiously behind him. The Trebitch group was by now in the third day of its slow-down strike. They came at night dragging their feet, the woman cooked the soup on a slow fire and they drank it with teaspoons. When connected labour branches joined them and bottle, brewery and nightclub workers staged one-and-a-half-minute warning strikes, the Central Committee of the Labour Federation saw itself forced to take emergency steps. They invited the capitalist to an informal meeting.

'Look here, Comrade Steiner,' they explained to him, 'this quarrel is over trifles, really. Why don't you want to increase a little that part of Comrade Trebitch's salary about which the comrades at the Income Tax know nothing? You can get mattresses, blankets, a porter and dogs from the development budget, and as for pensions, by the time those workers reach pensionable age, you'll long ago have lost control of the plant, so why worry?'

'It's a question of prestige,' Comrade Steiner replied. 'Rid me of this gang and I'll include you in my prayers.'

'We shall agree to the cancellation of the night watch only if it can be proved beyond the shadow of a doubt that it has become superfluous. But for that the whole plant will obviously have to switch over to night work.'

Thus Israel Corks Ltd turned to producing at night, switching its full complement of employees to a single night shift which comprised six workers, the secretary and Mr Steiner himself. At first certain difficulties arose over attendance at night school and cultural events, but with the help of certain technical improvements and a very long-term government loan, the management succeeded in fixing the price of the export corks at IL1 each. Tempers calmed down and production returned to normal.

Until one night, a few minutes after midnight, Mr Steiner called into his office the head of the workers' council.

'The plant is completely unsupervised all day long,' Mr Steiner said. 'Though this does not concern you, Ginzburg, for the sake of good order I hereby notify you that the management has decided to hire a watchman.'

We are a somewhat nervous people. We also have a very nice explanation for our edginess: For ages the nations of the world have found their chief pastime in inventing clever ways of driving us nuts. Lately they invented the telephone. It was a dirty trick, I must say.

Dial Dr Murder

One evening last week I was sitting in my study when suddenly the phone rang. What else could I do? I answered it.

'Hello.'

'Is Kalman there?' a male voice asked.

'Which Kalman?'

'Idiot!' the man snorted and hung up.

I was left alone and upset. Why does he hate me? Just because I'm not Kalman? Anyone who is not Kalman is necessarily an idiot? Am I to blame if he doesn't know how to dial? As a matter of fact, it's he who is an idiot! Yes, he! He!

I could feel the blood rushing to my head. What's the matter with him? Who does he think he is? What does he think he is? I took the receiver and dialled at random.

'Hello,' someone answered.

'What hello,' I roared, 'stupid!'

That felt good. The tornado in my head subsided, life returned to normal. Then my phone rang again.

'Hello!'

'Damn it, it's you again!' the Kalman seeker shouted. 'Get off my line, you ass!'

That made me lose control completely. I am an ass? I'll show him who is an ass!

I dialled 2–2 and four other sure-fire figures.

'Yes?' a voice piped in my ear.

'Swine,' I descended on him, 'miserable crook!'

'Yoel?' my victim asked.

'No!' I screamed. 'You'll come to a sad end, you moron! Go to hell, but quick!'

By then I had worked up a fine temper. Light-fingered, I sent out several more calls. A hoarse voice got a dressing down he won't forget for the rest of his life. One sucker protested, so I told him: 'You were a fool, Avigdor, and you are still a fool!' It sounded quite good, I must say. A woman who crossed my electronic path started sobbing. What can I do? They swear at me as well.

At the end of the series there was another ring:

'Hello,' I called, 'Kalman yourself, you dishrag, drop dead!'

But it was the hoarse one, I recognized his voice on the spot.

'Stupid,' he shrieked, 'the devil take you!'

I paid him back in kind. Without losing any time I made a dozen anonymous calls. Less than fifteen minutes passed before one of them ('maniac') called me back (he called me 'horse thief' – unimaginative). My phone rang all evening. The city came to life. We are a somewhat nervous people, it seems. It's the climate, probably.

The rule of the child in the Israeli family is not absolute, after all. The family strong man is naturally the baby-sitter, whose orders can never be appealed. At present a bill is being drafted to protect the parents' social rights. Until this bill is passed, the baby-sitter can fire the parents without severance pay for the slightest infringement of discipline.

The Economics of Baby-sitting

I think it is quite superfluous to introduce Regina Fleisch-hacker. By common consent, she is the best-qualified baby-sitter in the National League, a real pearl: punctual, loyal, soft-spoken, a wizard with the diapers. Baby Amir has never yet had reason to complain of her. There is only one flaw in Mrs Fleischhacker's otherwise consummate perfection: she lives in Tel Giborim, in the heart of the Holon wilderness, and therefore has no direct connection with our place. She has to travel by shuttle-taxi, which in Hebrew is called 'sherut', to the Central Bus Station and there to switch to another sherut, and sometimes there is no sherut and she has to squeeze her bulk into a jam-packed, slow-motion bus, and on such occasions she arrived in a state of near collapse, her eyes full of mute repoach.

'Again, no sherut.'

So round about 8.00 p.m. we always start praying that there should be a sherut and sometimes it helps. But we are terribly anxious about the future, because there is no substitute for Regina Fleischhacker. If only she would not live in Tel Giborim, without a phone.

What is this long introduction leading up to?

Well, it leads up to a certain evening when we planned to leave at 8.30 for the late show. On that same evening at sundown I had started writing a series of personal and most urgent letters, and because of the humidity my style did not flow as smoothly as it should have. At 8.30 the seasoned baby-sitter arrived and her eyes clearly told us that again there had been no sherut.

'I ran,' she panted, 'I ran like a madwoman.'

In such cases, the correct and tactful thing to do is storm out of the house, in order to justify the mad baby-sitter's marathon dash. But, as I said, the urgent letters were not yet finished, I was still working on them. And, indeed, a few minutes later the door of my study flew open.

'You are still here?'

'Just a second . . .'

'Then why must I run like a madwoman, if you have all the time in the world?'

'We're . . . we're ready.'

'Why call me at all if you're staying home?'

'We'll pay . . . even if . . .'

'No need to pay, ma'am!' Thus Regina Fleischhacker majestically. 'I don't take money for the time I don't work! Next time kindly think twice before you call me!'

Without further ado I grabbed my typewriter and we fled out of the house. I finished the letters at the pastry shop across the street. The typing caused a mild sensation, but gradually people got accustomed to it.

Naturally, we did not make it to the cinema that night. My little wife, that born Realpolitiker, proposed that we kill the three-hour minimum of the professional baby-sitter strolling in the city's streets. Tel Aviv is beautiful at night. Especially on the seashore, the northern suburbs, Jaffa and the Abu Kabir Plain. We returned at midnight on our last legs and paid the prescribed IL5.75.

'When will you be needing me again?' Regina asked, her eyebrows raised.

The little woman looked at me, expecting a snap decision. Yet any mistake would have been fatal because Mrs Fleischhacker has no phone, so that a date once made cannot be cancelled. She lived in Tel Giborim, remember, and lacked direct communications.

'Day after tomorrow? At eight?'

'All right,' I mumbled. 'I think . . . we'll go to the movies.'

Hidden are the ways of the Almighty.

On that day after tomorrow, at 7.00 p.m., my back started aching something awful. I think I even ran a temperature. My faithful wife stood at my bedside, greatly concerned.

'You've got to get up.' She snapped her fingers. 'She'll be here any moment now and we've got to go.'

'But I'm sick!'

'Make an effort, for goodness' sake! It will be terribly embarrassing if she sees that she again came all the way from Tel Giborim for nothing.'

'I'm dizzy.'

'So am I. Take an aspirin. Come on, get up.'

Regina, that walking Swiss chronometer, arrived at eight sharp, breathing heavily.

'Shalom,' she hissed, 'again there was no . . .'

I dressed in a panic. If there had been a sherut, we might conceivably have started negotiations, but like this, what with buses and all, organized resistance was out of the question. We left in a hurry. Outside, I fell against the wall, too weak to stand on my legs. I felt lousy, really – it must have been flu or something. What was to be done? The cinema was out of the question in such a state.

We got into our car and I stretched out on the rear seat. I'm rather tall and our car is small. 'O Lord,' I wailed, 'why do I have to crouch here in our car with the grippe almost killing me, why?' The Lord did not answer my query and besides I am also blessed with a tinge of claustrophobia. The crisis drew to a head seventy-five minutes later.

'Woman,' I whispered, 'I'm turning in.'

'Already?' the little one exclaimed in the car's clammy darkness. 'Only an hour and a half. Do you expect her to come all the way from Tel Giborim for so little?'

'I don't expect her to do anything,' I croaked. 'Only I don't want to die for Mrs Fleischhacker. I'm still young, life is beautiful. I'm turning in, woman.'

'Come on, wait another twenty minutes.'

'I can't.'

'You know what?' the little one caught up with me in front of the entrance. 'Let's try and slip in without her hearing us. We'll sit quietly in our bedroom and wait.'

That sounded reasonable. I agreed. We opened the door slowly and tiptoed in. A shaft of light came from my study. So that's where Fleischhacker was. We advanced cautiously, taking advantage of every irregularity in the well-known terrain, but a few steps before the objective, misfortune struck.

'Who's there?' Regina roared from my study. 'Who goes there?'

We turned on the light.

'It's us,' the wife quickly called out. 'Ephraim forgot the present.'

What present? The wife threw me a menacing glance, walked up to the bookshelf and after hesitating for just the fraction of a second, pulled out the *History of the English Theatre, 1616–1985*. Then we said 'Sorry' and exited with the book. In front of the door I felt faint, and for the first time red polka dots appeared before my eyes. One of my molars also started hurting. I sat down on the curb and, if memory serves me, started sobbing.

'It was our only chance.' The wife passed her cool hand over my burning brow. 'In an hour or two we'll be able to turn in.'

'If only I survive,' I took an oath, 'we'll move to Tel Giborim, across the street from Mrs Fleischhacker.'

Half an hour later I informed my wife that I was ready for another try.

This time it worked.

Our previous experience in self-infiltration stood us well. The door fell shut with the lightest of clicks, the light in the study was still burning bright. We made the bedroom according to plan, closed the sliding doors with feeling, stretched out on our beds and waited for the three hours to pass.

As for the sequel, there is a certain gap in my memory.

'Ephraim,' I suddenly heard my little wife's voice as from a distance, 'it's five thirty!'

She also shook me with all her might. I blinked in the strong light coming through the windows. It had been a long time since I last enjoyed such refreshing sleep. Our strategic position, on the other hand, was deplorable.

'We've got to get Regina out of there,' the little one mused. 'Wait . . .'

With that she went out and slipped into Amir's adjacent room. Two tense seconds later the baby's high-frequency yells almost cracked the walls. The wife sprinted back.

'Did you pinch him?'

'Of course.'

Regina Fleischhacker's heavy body hurtled towards the nursery like a flash. We took advantage of the commotion, made for the front door, went out and came back through it, calling loudly:

'Good morning!'

'Is this a time to come home?' a bleary-eyed Regina asked, cradling an angry Amir in her arms. 'Where have you been?'

'At an orgy.'

'Today's youth!' Regina shook her head and presented the bill. Then she stepped out into the cool morning to look for a sherut to Tel Giborim. I bet you she didn't find one.

An uncle of mine, a politician by profession, once said to me: 'Son, never join a ruling party which has only a nominal majority.' That's why I luckily became a writer. Indeed, the above axiom proves itself almost daily: in our parliament, which in Hebrew is called 'Knesset', the oppressed slaves of the ruling party do not dare to leave the meeting hall for any reason whatsoever lest they endanger the government majority in the next vote. That's what the poet meant when he wrote: 'All hands are needed at harvest time.'

The Unsung Hero

The following story is devoted to the unknown soldiers of Israel's democracy, to that handful of elected representatives who fulfil their duty to nation and party with a loyalty beyond the call of duty.

More specifically, this is the story of Knesset Member I. L. Slutzkovski.

The time: two days before the Knesset vote on the controversial air-pollution bill. In view of the bill's deep moral implications, it was decided for once to permit the MK's to cross party lines and to vote according to their consciences; that is to say, an agreement was concluded according to which in each party two members would be guided by their private consciences, and one would abstain. Furthermore, each side was apportioned an equal number of Arab MK's. And, last but not least, it was agreed between the government party and the Liberals that, for reasons of economy, each of them would leave one representative abroad: MK Dr Bar-Bitzua, just then visiting his dentist in Stockholm, and the government emissary, MK I. L. Slutzkovski, representing us at the Socialist Congress of the Headhunters of New Guinea.

The bomb exploded at the headquarters of the ruling party exactly thirty-six hours before the fateful vote.

The big electronic brain at HQ which, coupled with long-range radar, tracks the 120 MK's twenty-four hours a day all over the globe, set off a warning buzzer on the master console. The blip on the map of Europe signalling Liberal Dr Bar-Bitzua's whereabouts had suddenly started moving in a southerly direction. At daybreak the blip reached the border of the Fail-Safe Zone. The alert went out that as from that moment the hostile MK could make it to the balloting.

Five minutes later the complete emergency crew was chairborne and direct contact was established with the High Command. The red phone jangled on the Prime Minister's desk.

'Dr Bar-Bitzua landed in Rome at dawn,' he was informed. 'The Liberals have broken the agreement in order to win the vote. What shall we do?'

'Have Slutzkovski come at once!'

The cable from the Israel Consul in Kokoda made it doubtful whether an adequate level of air pollution could be maintained in this country. I. L. Slutzkovski had set out for the Socialist Congress through the jungle, but in the meantime a typhoon had struck the island, making roads impassable to the extent that not even his salary could be sent after him, not to mention a message.

Every single operative at 110 Hayarkon realized what this meant: should the government fail to line up a majority, it would have to resign, anarchy would grip the country, tension would increase in the area, possibly a regional war, an inter-bloc clash, atoms, Armageddon.

The Operations Branch officers watched the Knessetoscope with growing alarm. The Bar-Bitzua blip was now nearing Cyprus, while that of I.L. Slutzkovski was still hovering futilely over the Bulawayo range. Without further delay, an unequivocal order was flashed to the Kokoda Consulate:

'Find Parrot regardless of cost.'

'Parrot' was Slutzkovski's code name in the operation. The Consul worked his connections with the aborigines and soon the big jungle drums were disturbing the island's quiet – two long throbs, three short thumps. . . .

'White-tiger-who-always-tells-stale-jokes-return-at-once-to-King-for-show-of-hands. Over!'

Thus the urgent message of the Workers' Party of Israel was passed on from village to village. It reached Slutzkovski a day later on the banks of the Dorinoco.

'Bwana,' the chief porter brought him the disconcerting news, 'the tom-toms say Bwana has to go to 110 Hayarkon Street beyond the mountains or else.'

'Oy!' Slutzkovski jumped up and rallied his men. 'Get up, lazybones! We're returning to Kokoda!'

'Bwana, we won't budge from here,' the head porter protested. 'The jungle tribes are on the warpath.'

'All right,' I. L. Slutzkovski said, 'then I'll return by myself!'

Slutzkovski set out in a dug-out, but the primitive craft soon capsized and Parrot continued swimming. A posse of crocodiles trailed him for a while, but his awful swearing scared them off. He spent the night on the bank of the river, among the bamboo reeds. At about midnight a savage headhunter jumped on him from a coconut tree, but Slutzkovski produced his Knesset card and proved his immunity. On the way to the Dutch border post he was attacked by a black panther, but outran it. He reached the outpost at the end of his tether and collapsed.

'To Jerusalem,' his parched lips whispered, 'for the voting . . .'

Jungle fever had completely sapped his strength and it looked as if he would never recover. International solidarity saved him. The May Day message from the jungle outpost was monitored by a Siamese student, then transmitted by an Indian radio ham to a Serbian pharmacist, then to a Cypriot archbishop, and finally reached the Israel Broadcasting Station, where it was mislaid. All this wireless traffic had wasted an awful lot of time, but it did not matter. Slutzkovski had in the meantime been flown to Bombay by American helicopter.

Tension in Hayarkon Street was well-nigh unbearable. It was decided to have the Prime Minister embark on a filibuster, so as to gain time. Who knows, maybe . . .

At 8.30 in the morning the teleprinter started clacking: 'Parrot's bus was involved in a fatal road accident on the border of Afghanistan. It caught fire and all passengers died, except for I. L. Slutzkovski, that dyed-in-the-wool party man. When last seen he was trying to get a ride to Iran.'

To compound the disaster, it was discovered that M. Sulzbaum, MK – whose request for an appointment to the Finance Committee had been rejected – had vanished.

Two hours to the vote.

Slutzkovski reached the outskirts of Teheran completely worn out by the long walk. He found the Israel Legation deserted, as all the officials were out searching for him. He phoned Hayarkon.

'Slutzki!' they shouted at the other end of the line. 'They're voting in an hour's time. Fly here, for God's sake, fly!'

Taking advantage of the dawn mist, I.L. Slutzkovski slunk into the jetliner parked on the runway of Teheran Airport. He started the engines by intuition and took off into the rising sun. Two Persian fighter planes took off in pursuit, but collided at eight thousand feet. Over Upper Galilee the plane ran out of gas. Slutzkovski jumped out of it and got caught in the branches of a tree near Nazareth. A traffic cop freed him and gave him a ticket for jumping without a parachute.

The Prime Minister was not yet through with his marathon speech holding up the voting. He interspersed his remarks with amusing anecdotes and also gave a completely comprehensive historical review. The Opposition was becoming restive. Dr Bar-Bitzua cut a pitiful figure in the Liberal benches, his swollen jaws proof of his aching teeth, his right arm secured by a rope the other end of which was held by the party whip. At the very last moment the Coalition had freed M. Sulzbaum from the washroom in which mysterious hands had locked him. But one vote was still missing. . . .

An urgent message reached the Prime Minister in the middle of his speech:

'Slutzkovski's taxi was struck by lightning near Zichron.'

The safety-belt appeal contributed twenty precious minutes, but not more. The Opposition waived its right to reply. *The vote* . . .

The Speaker is counting hands.

The Party Secretary, who has dragged Slutzkovski from Zichron by the scruff of his neck, is storming up the stairs.

Speaker: 'The Opposition has fifty-six votes and one Member is asleep. The Government has fifty –'

Crash!

A mighty kick breaks down the door. Slutzkovski falls in, his arm raised.

'Fifty-seven votes for the Government,' the Speaker sums up. 'The bill is defeated. Bye.'

Tourism is the world's best business, especially in a country where only the time differential prevented Moses, Jesus and Mohammed from holding a symposium on the subject 'Monotheism and Its Influence on the Flow of Tourists'. In line with this concept we have a special ministry for the encouragement of tourism, which patiently explains to the population that we have to handle our foreign guests with exceptional courtesy, even though this may cause some discomfort here and there. As a matter of fact, the courtesy business has not yet quite come off, but the discomfort has been fully implemented.

The Tourist Blitz

Humidity. They say it's mainly the humidity which drives them to the cooler North. They crawl around, sweating and sticky, through Tel Aviv's narrow, steaming alleyways, and the only thing which keeps them alive is the thought of the marvellous week-end they will spend on the shores of the Kinneret. So we booked a double room at the largest hotel in Tiberias and sighed, greatly relieved.

We arrived at our destination in excellent spirits, knowing that the above establishment is the exclusive spa's most exclusive inn, its rooms spacious, deeply cooled and sybaritically comfortable. In short, we prepared to feel kings for a day.

But we sensed a certain coolness in the manner of the reception clerk.

'Sorry,' he apologized on behalf of the management, 'sorry, but a group of tourists from the Winegrowers' Conference are due at our hotel, so we cannot offer you, sir or ma'am, a room, except in the old wing, and even that cubbyhole has to be vacated by noon tomorrow, unless you don't mind being thrown out bodily. We are sure you understand our difficult position, sir.'

'I protest,' I protested. 'My money is as good as the tourists', isn't it?'

'Who's talking about money?' the desk cut us short. 'It is our patriotic duty to make the stay of these tourists as pleasant as possible. Besides, they give bigger tips. So get moving, but quick!'

We hurried down the old wing, lest we give him a pretext to kicking us out. After all, desk is desk and not just plain anybody. Our little room was somewhat stuffy, but good enough for the natives. We unpacked, then with springy, careless steps sauntered off for a Kinneret swim. One of the deputy managers intercepted us.

'Why are you loafing about here?' He frowned at us. 'The tourists are due any moment. Back to your kennels!'

We drew in our tails and hurried back to base, but by then a sentry had been placed in front of our door. It appears that tourists from the Peashooter Congress were also due. Our luggage had been moved to the nether regions, next to the boiler room.

'You can rest here until eleven,' said the sentry, who at heart was a decent chap, 'but don't use the hot water, the tourists need it.'

By then we dared move through the corridors only by hugging the walls, and a deep inferiority complex had gripped us.

'Do you think they'll flog us, or something?' the wife whispered, but I assured her that as long as we cooperated with the desk we were not in any immediate physical danger. Only once did we see some sort of manager patrolling the Israeli quarters with a cat-o'-nine-tails, but we carefully avoided him. After lunch we had a nap on our pallet, but were awakened by the din of an arriving motorized column. We peeped out through a crack in the wall and saw about a dozen luxurious buses, each containing a complete conference. We made a quick appraisal of the situation. I called the desk.

'To the sub-basement?'

'At the double!'

We moved down to the oubliettes. It was quite pleasant, except for the bats. The dinner tray was slipped under our door. Ready for all eventualities, we did not undress, expecting more tourists to arrive. And indeed, at midnight they moved us again, this time on to a raft on the lake. Actually, we were lucky in getting an almost new raft. The other hapless natives got just a few planks and logs.

Three drowned. Fortunately, the tourists didn't notice.

Our people's attachment to the land is proverbial. We have periods when we all buy land, or at least plots in the city. It's said that this is also good business. In times of prosperity the price of plots jumps by IL35 a day – that is, IL1.50 per hour or 2.5 agorot per minute. You buy a plot on the northern outskirts of Tel Aviv, wait for two years and by then the plot is worth a hundred times more because it is now in the centre of the expanding city. But then you have to sell in a hurry because in another two years the very same plot will again be on the outskirts of Tel Aviv – the southern outskirts.

Cry, the Beloved Real Estate

It is no secret that nowadays the most rewarding racket is to buy and sell real estate. Of course, you can also make nice money by working, but hawking plots is much more profitable.

A naïve person may well ask: Then why do people work all the same, instead of speculating in real estate?

The answer is quite simple: No one works. Everybody speculates in real estate.

So much for generalities. This is where the little woman steps into the picture.

'Everybody is getting rich,' her words, 'only you sit there and scribble-scrabble like a half-wit. Buy a plot!'

'All right,' thus I, 'where?'

'What does it matter? Just buy.'

'And the money?'

'From your salary.'

'With that you could hardly buy enough land to park Rafi's bicycle.'

'So we'll sell the apartment. With the proceeds we'll buy a plot. In a few months' time we'll sell the plot, buy back the apartment plus another plot.'

'And where shall we live in the meantime?'

'In a tabernacle.'

That sounded reasonable. After all, a man cannot remain indifferent to changing social patterns. We decided not to waste any money on brokers but trust our own judgement. I went to the suburb of the Big Shots which, topography-wise, is nearest to Helsingfors Street, picked a lovely plot in the centre with lots of shade and called on the owner of the plot, a little clerk at the Municipality who four years ago had been forced to buy it in monthly instalments of IL3.

'For such a plot,' the little clerk told me, 'They pay as a rule 45,000 pounds.'

'45,000 pounds?'

'That was some time ago. Nowadays the price is IL50,000. You want to buy, yes or no? Make up your mind, will you!'

'I want to ring my wife.'

'All right, I'll give you fifteen minutes.'

Nothing came of it because our phone was engaged, and in fifteen minutes' time the prices had gone up anyway. But all night long regret would not let us sleep. We counted the hours and with chattering teeth multiplied them by IL1.50. When we reached IL12 I jumped out of my bed and, panic-stricken, rushed over to the little clerk. Too late, alas! At dawn he had sold the plot to the milkman.

We sent out feelers towards the Ramat Aviv badlands. I found a cosy plot on half a dunam for only 25,000 but unfortunately this price included a luxury villa as well, and that I did not like, because to demolish it would have cost a fortune, to say nothing of the bother. Who has time for that? The price of plots keeps rising. That's real estate for you!

Reluctantly, we decided to consult a broker after all. Someone recommended the well-known real estate broker Victor Stockler. I contacted him. Two days later he gave me a ring.

'I got it,' Stockler informed me. 'Three quarters of a dunam of level ground in Afeka – 28,000.'

'28,000?'

'That's most reasonable. A fantastic place with a school right next door. Don't decide right away. I'll hold your option until tomorrow.'

At home we made a quick reckoning: in the afternoon we'll sell the apartment, the car and the film rights to this story, then in the morning we'll take out a loan – yes, we'll make it. In two months' time we'll dispose of Afeka and make a profit of IL14,000 on it. Child's play, really. Next day I informed Stockler in an emotion-laden voice:

'I'll buy the Afeka thing!'

'Sorry,' thus Stockler. 'It's sold.'

'And the option?'

'Was fictitious. I was offered 29,000 in the meantime. You have to make up your mind fast in this business, sir.'

That's real estate for you. The tempo is dizzying. The story is told of a Zichron driver who for 100,000 bought a big plot from a sub-contractor. They went to clinch the deal at a nearby kiosk, and after the first glass of juice the sub-contractor suddenly said: 'You know what? Sell me back the plot.' The driver asked 120,000. The sub-contractor plunked down 15,000 in cash and the driver took it. They had another glass and parted, well satisfied. That's real estate, gentlemen. No hanky panky there.

Last Thursday another broker rang me up.

'There's a half-dunam bargain here in Tel Baruch. A fantastic spot, not a school within ten miles! Interested?'

'Hold it! I'm coming!'

I rushed down the stairs five at a time, drove to Tel Baruch at an excessive speed, skip-hop-jumped out of the car in front of a breathtaking plot of land and suddenly felt the bottom falling out of my world. There was that grabbing cheat of a broker sitting astride a rock, counting a ten-inch stack of banknotes.

'Sechsundreissig toisend vierhundert fufzig,' he counted. 'I sold out ten minutes ago to a passer-by, sechsundreissig toisend vierhundert sechzig . . .'

This was no laughing matter. Prices go up all the time. You have to make up your mind on the spot, otherwise you'll always miss the boat.

Stockler rang up at midnight. He was in a fine state of excitement.

'I got something exceptional in Herzliya Pituah. A whole dunam next to the communal hall which they'll never build. Wonderful scenery guaranteed.'

'Stop!' I screamed. 'I'll buy it!'

'Sorry,' Stockler answered, 'it's sold.'

He promised to ring again should there be anything for me. Since then I have been sitting next to the phone, my hand extended in readiness, breathlessly waiting for the exhilarating ring. Yesterday at dusk, at long last, there was a strong, encouraging ring. I quickly grabbed the receiver and shouted into it: 'I'm buying!' Thereupon someone at the other end of the line quietly replaced the receiver and scurried away on tiptoe. You have to be quick on the draw if you want to succeed in real estate.

'Love thy neighbour as thyself', the absurd Hebrew commandment goes, meaning you shouldn't do to your fellow man what you wouldn't have him do to you. A nice law, universally respected. In any case, on the strength of this law, never give a loan to your friends, good people, because clearly you wouldn't like to owe money to anyone, would you?

The Insult and the Injury

September 7. Today I ran into Adalbert Toscanini in the Passage. He looked extremely upset. It seems that he has asked Bialazurkevitz to lend him IL100 just for a few days and that skunk, that monster, that heel, that rabid dog was not ashamed to say to him: 'I've got them, but you can't have them!' Now he can wait until Adalbert will speak to him again.

So that's how low we have sunk! There is not a shred of common decency left in this rotten world. 'Yes, there is,' I said, and there and then handed over the wretched IL100 to Toscanini. 'At last a human being,' Adalbert whispered, choking back his tears. 'I'll return them within a fortnight, rest assured.'

According to the wife, I am an idiot. I explained to her: 'I didn't want to make an enemy of Toscanini.'

September 18. Ran into Adalbert on Allenby Road. We walked side by side for a few steps and I meticulously avoided mentioning the loan. But Toscanini lost his temper and hissed at me: 'Don't lose any sleep, you'll get your money back, down to the last agor! I promised to repay you within two weeks, the two weeks are not yet over, so what the hell do you want?' I told him it really was not worth getting upset over such a trifle, whereupon Toscanini remarked that I was no better than the rest and turned his back on me.

October 3. A very painful incident at the Rio Café. Adalbert Toscanini was sitting at one of the tables with Bialazurkevitz and did not take his eyes off me for a second. He was visibly seething with anger. I tried to look pleasant, but this only added fuel to the fire. After a while Adalbert got up from his table and strode over to me: 'Grossartig!' he shouted, so that everybody should hear him. 'So I am a few days late repaying, is that the end of the world? Don't look at me as if I were a murderer!' I said God forbid, whereupon he answered something rude which does not bear printer's ink. I think there are going to be complications. The wife warned me: 'Didn't I tell you? You'll see, there's even going to be violence.'

October 11. According to reliable information reaching me, Toscanini is spreading rumours all over the city to the effect that I am a hopeless drug addict, and that two well-known female lawyers have started paternity suits against me. Needless to say, there is not a shred of truth in all this. I don't even smoke. All the same, the wife opines that for the sake of my mental peace I ought to waive those IL100.

October 14. Today I met Adalbert in the queue at the movies. His face was livid. His eyes burned red in their sockets, his neck muscles were unnaturally taut. 'Look, Adalbert,' I said to him good-naturedly, 'in view of the difficult economic situation, let's forget about that money, is that all right?' Toscanini flared up: 'Forget nothing,' he roared. 'I don't need your generosity! What do you take me for – a dishrag?' I have never seen him so upset. Bialazurkevitz, with whom he was going to the cinema, had to hold him, otherwise he would have thrown himself on me. I ran straight home. The woman: 'Didn't I tell you so?'

October 29. Several people today asked me whether it was true that I had signed up with the Red Guards but had been rejected as a weakling. An utter fabrication, of course. I know only too well who is behind these rumours. Last week my windows were pelted with anonymous rocks. The whole city is talking about the life-and-death struggle going on between Toscanini and myself. Two days ago, as I came into the Rio, Toscanini jumped up and started shouting: 'May anyone come in here? What is this, a refuge for bums?' The owner pushed me out of the door, to avoid unpleasantness. 'Dirty miser!'

Adalbert blazed after me. 'Bloodsucker!' The wife had said so.

November 8. Today Aladar, my favourite cousin, called on us and asked me to lend him just IL10. 'I've got them, but you can't have them!' I said to him. 'Get out!' I like the boy and don't want to spoil our friendship. I've got enough trouble as it is with the Ministry of the Interior. Someone denounced me, saying I have an Aryan grandmother, and they took away my passport. So much for my plan to flee abroad. The wife, whose warning it will be remembered I had ignored, does not let me go outdoors by myself.

I went to see a psychiatrist: 'Because of his strong feeling of guilt, Adalbert Toscanini hates you, sir,' he explained. 'A typical father complex which can be relieved only by the proverbial patricide, as a sort of conciliatory offering. A very clear case.' I pointed out to him that I was still young, full of vitality. The psychiatrist informed me that Toscanini's all-consuming, mortal hatred would go on burning bright for as long as his loan still stood – that is, as long as he is unable to repay it. 'Couldn't you send him some money anonymously?' I rushed to the bank, withdrew IL500 and dropped them into Toscanini's letterbox.

November 11. Today I met Adalbert on Allenby Road. He spat on the ground and walked on. I reported to the psychiatrist. 'Well,' he said, 'we tried, we failed.' From a most reliable source I learned that Adalbert has bought a doll bearing a striking resemblance to me and is now sticking pins into it every morning. The police won't intervene. Pinpricks in my back.

November 20. Shouts outside last night. 'O Lord,' I prayed on my bed of pain. 'I have erred horribly, I lent money to a pal in Israel! Will I have to bear the terrible consequences of my madness to the end of my days? Is there no way out of my predicament?' I heard a deep, fatherly voice coming from above: 'None.'

December 1. Pinpricks have spread to my chest as well. Leaning heavily on my wife, I dragged my sick body, that victim of the father complex, to a reputable doctor. At the corner we bumped into Bialazurkevitz. 'Ephraim,' the wife whispered, 'he is an ideal father figure. Look at his head, a typical father head.' A faint glimmer of hope.

December 3. I accosted Toscanini in front of the Rio. 'Thanks for the money,' I quickly said to him before he could knock me down. 'Bialazurkevitz has paid me your whole debt. True, he asked me not to tell you, but I think you deserve to know what a friend you have. So from now on, it's not to me you owe that money, but to Bialazurkevitz.' Adalbert's hard face relaxed: 'Bialazurkevitz is a real pal,' he whispered, choking back the tears. 'I'll repay him in a few days.'

I am saved!

January 22. As we walked arm in arm through the Passage, Adalbert said to me: 'Bialazurkevitz, that rabid dog, has been looking at me these last few days in such a way that I could slap his face. True, I owe him money, but that does not yet make me his dishrag. His little game is going to have a very sad ending!'

But that is no longer my business.

Every schoolboy knows that the Orient is a hot-bed of genuine hospitality. It is said that noble Bedouin sheikhs may have you a whole year in their tent without giving you even the slightest hint that perhaps it is time to beat it. Unfortunately, the number of noble Bedouin sheikhs among Tel Aviv waiters is strictly limited.

Closing Time

The time was 11.30 p.m. and we did not yet feel like hitting the sack. We had just seen a very vulgar show and were itching to start the post-mortem. We walked a few steps up moonlit Dizengoff Street and decided to end the pleasant evening in an appropriate way.

'Come,' the wife proposed, 'let's have a glass of tea.'

We entered the first restaurant we came across. It was a small but intimate spot, with coloured fluorescent lights, a shining espresso machine and two undressing waiters. The only other person present was a bald man who wiped the bar counter with a dirty rag. As we came in, he looked at his watch and said something to one of the waiters, who thereupon slipped again into his time-worn white jacket. The air was fraught with social ferment, but we ignored it and resolutely sat down at one of the tables.

'Tea,' I sang out. 'Two teas!'

The waiter appeared to hesitate for a few seconds, then stepped into the kitchen. We heard him ask behind the door, his voice filled with hatred:

'Any boiling water left?'

Meanwhile the waiter had started folding the tables outside. He did this with clipped movements and staccato noise, as if underscoring the ruthless flight of time. The first waiter came running with two glasses of tea and plunked them down on our table, an irritated expression on his face. We stirred the tea for a while, hoping to warm it up a degree or two, then started discussing the vulgar show.

'Pardon me . . .'

It was Baldhead. He lifted our glasses and removed the much-spotted cover from the table. We did not mind, because the rough-grained, coffee-etched tabletop looked quite pleasant to the eye, but in the meantime the first waiter had taken off his white coat and was now standing in a blue raincoat at the doorway, waiting. The second waiter finished the folding and turned off the neon sign outside.

A certain uneasiness gripped us.

'Could it be,' I whispered to the little one, 'could it be that they want us to go?'

'Maybe,' the wife replied. 'Don't look!'

The tension rose by leaps and bounds. Obviously, any sign of weakness would have been fatal in this situation, so we went on whispering excitedly at our isolated table. Soon afterwards the raincoated waiter sidled up and held a plate with the bill under my nose. I pushed the piece of chinaware aside and Raincoat retreated. Baldhead took the little one's hat off the rack and delicately placed it on our table.

'Thank you,' the little one said to him. 'Have you got cakes?'

Baldhead shuddered and looked backward at the second waiter, who was combing his hair in front of the mirror. The silence lasted for what seemed an eternity, but in the end one of the waiters, the raincoated one, threw down in front of us a nondescript cheesy something. The little one dropped her fork and a new one had to be fetched. If looks could kill . . .

'I can't hold out much longer.'

'You must!'

The lights in the restaurant went off and on several times, but we took this, too, in our stride. Baldhead rang down an iron shutter with an ear-shattering bang, then locked the courtyard door, turning the key twice with ominous finality. A grimy old crone slouched in from the kitchen carrying bucket and ragmop and started scrubbing the floor.

'Watch out, ma'am.'

With that the old lady pushed the ragmop under our table. We raised our legs high so as to afford her access. The well-combed waiter in the meantime walked through the restaurant, lifted the chairs and placed them upside down atop the tables. By then we felt clearly that we were *persona non grata*.

'But,' I whispered to the little one, 'why don't they tell us to go?'

'It embarrasses them,' the wife informed me. 'They are trying to be polite.'

Through half-lowered eyelids I surveyed the field. The first waiter was standing out in the street, watching us. The other waiter had just about finished upturning the chairs. Baldhead put on a black beret and opened a small cupboard on the wall. The lights went out in a flash and only a little moonlight filtered in through the door. Then I felt someone placing a chair on my back. I groped in the darkness for the wife's hand. Those were climactic moments.

'I say,' I heard the wife's voice, 'have you got magazines?'

That was the proverbial straw. For a brief while one could feel the air quivering, then Baldhead struck a match and came over to us from the door.

'Excuse me, he said, and his face was flushed in the flickering light, 'we close at midnight.'

'Then why didn't you say so?' I asked. 'How could we have guessed?'

We brushed the chairs off our backs, paid and left, skidding on the wet floor tiles. The time was 11.48, Eastern Mediterranean Time.

Our country is at present in the dangerous stage of intensive industrial development. If a week passes without the opening of at least one tyre plant, our Finance Minister feels a terrible emptiness at the pit of his stomach. It is said that he is afflicted with a severe case of what is known as the country-development syndrome.

Economist and Poet

FINANCE MINISTER: What else?

ADVISERS: The Ministry of Education and Culture has been recommending for eighteen months that we should award a subsidy of IL75,000 to the new opera ensemble. 'This new company,' the report says, 'has proved itself a most valuable musical asset, whose contribution to the country's cultural life – '

FINANCE MINISTER: Just a second, gentlemen, this is not the Cultural Council but the Treasury, if I'm not mistaken!

ADVISERS: The ensemble has submitted seven applications, so far.

FINANCE MINISTER: They can submit ten, for all I care! They think that the State Treasury is a milch cow, to be milked by any flopping show troupe! The cheek to ask for a subsidy!

ADVISERS: Operas as a rule appeal to a limited audience of art lovers, and it is only natural that they should be subsidized.

FINANCE MINISTER: Gentlemen, let the figures talk! How many times do they perform an opera?

ADVISERS: About forty times.

FINANCE MINISTER: How many seats are there in the hall?

ADVISERS: 483, but it's not always a full house.

FINANCE MINISTER: Thank you, that's all I wanted to know! Forty times 483 are 19,320, less the empty seats. With such a miserable showing, not even a choir has the right to exist! Besides, we already have an opera! Has that gentleman at least had the decency to consult the Productivity Institute?

ADVISERS: We don't think so.

FINANCE MINISTER: Just as I thought! It's so much easier to come running for subsidies to the government, isn't it? No, gentlemen, this is not the way to build up the state. Let that stuck-up ensemble introduce efficiency methods at all levels of their performance and services, let them lower the cost price and commission on their tickets, until they become competitive with other theatres.

ADVISERS: Yes. But the ensemble has been an outstanding critical success.

FINANCE MINISTER: Don't make me lose my temper! When will our people at long last learn that only economically viable enterprises have a right to exist!

ADVISERS: That's true. Yet, from an artistic point of view . . .

FINANCE MINISTER: I'm not an artist, gentlemen, I'm an economist! Next! What else?

ADVISERS: We have here an offer from an Italian retailer of knitted goods, to establish a fibre-glass factory.

FINANCE MINISTER: Sounds good! The first Israeli fibreglass factory! Very nice!

ADVISERS: Very! Though there are already three such plants in Israel . . .

FINANCE MINISTER: So there should be room for one more!

ADVISERS: As a matter of fact, two of them closed down last month with a loss of three million.

FINANCE MINISTER: Gentlemen, please! Some things are above dry statistics.

ADVISERS: Certainly! The Italian retailer asks for a loan of nine millions, of which he undertakes to invest immediately five millions in the plant.

FINANCE MINISTER: Is he bringing in new machinery?

ADVISERS: We suppose so.

FINANCE MINISTER: Big, tall machines, yes?

ADVISERS: As a matter of fact, squat ones.

FINANCE MINISTER: But with wide pedestals! A new, praiseworthy initiative for our people: Hebrew fibre-glass competing on the world market! With the State Emblem stamped on it! Made in Israel! What's fibre-glass?

ADVISERS: Glass made of fibre.

FINANCE MINISTER: Who cares? Do I have to go into details when before our very eyes another outpost on our road to economic independence is being set up?

ADVISERS: That in any case, but what do we need —

FINANCE MINISTER: Gentlemen, I can hear the throbbing and humming of machinery joining the cycle of production. I can see dozens of craftsmen bursting into joyful song . . .

ADVISERS: Two closed down.

FINANCE MINISTER: Out of the machine's muzzle there emerges the marvellous thin thread, glimmering and flimmering in the sunshine like a golden fleece which heralds our nation's coming of age. . . . Faber-glass! I mean, fibre-glass!

ADVISERS: That's certainly true, but nine millions . . .

FINANCE MINISTER: Don't bother me with figures! Can't you see, this is music, gentlemen, new music, creative art, the future.

ADVISERS: From an economic point of view . . .

FINANCE MINISTER: I'm not an economist, gentlemen, I'm a poet!

'A Yiddishe Mama' is the famous song which epitomizes the Jewish mother's boundless love for her offspring. To be sure, we have no quarrel with that love. The question is only: how about the Daddy of that offspring – that is, the husband of the Mama? Let's take for example an ordinary citizen: Napoleon Bonaparte.

How Napoleon was Defeated

As the sun rose over the battlefields, the Emperor was already poring over the maps in the salon of the palace. The faithful marshals crowding around him were keeping respectfully quiet. The Greatest Commander of Men was drafting his final plans for the decisive clash with the Kings of Europe. The exile on Elba had left no traces on the Emperor's self-assurance; only his hair had become sparser and had acquired a hint of silver at the sides. In the distance one could hear some isolated cannon shots: Blücher's army was moving northwards to the fields of Waterloo.

The silken curtains were fluttering in the morning breeze. The world was watching with bated breath.

'Napoleon, your breakfast is ready!'

In the doorway appeared Sarah, the Emperor's third wife. A nice and devoted woman, her hair was gathered in a kerchief, and in her hand she held a dustrag. The Emperor had married her on Elba. It was said that she came from one of the better Jewish families on the island.

'Your food is getting cold,' the Empress called out. 'Come and have your breakfast, Napoleon, your friends here won't run away. It's the same story every day,' Sarah explained the situation to the marshals while picking things up in the salon. 'I keep asking him: Napoleon, do you want to eat or don't you want to eat, just tell me, but as soon as the meal is ready he always finds things to do, and I have to stand around and wait for hours. I can't warm up the dishes endlessly, the maid left the day before yesterday, and here I am all by myself with the kid. Napoleon, come and have your breakfast.'

'Just a second,' the Eagle mumbled and drew in the lines of deployment on the map. 'Just a second.'

The thunder of guns grew beyond the hills. Marshal Ney consulted his watch, slightly worried: the artillery of the Duke of Wellington was getting the range.

'I'm dropping on my feet,' Sarah observed. 'You leave your clothes scattered all over the place and I do nothing but hang them back in the wardrobe. And take your hand out of your coat, I told you the cloth is stretching and I can't press it back into shape. My husband has some habits fit to drive you mad! Come and have your breakfast, Napoleon.'

'I'm coming,' the Emperor answered and, tense-faced, turned towards his staff officers. 'Blücher and Wellington are trying to join their forces regardless of losses,' he analysed the strategic situation. 'Our mission will be to set up a barrier between them.'

'The food is getting stone cold.'

'We'll attack in an hour's time!'

The adjutant's heavy steps are heard approaching outside. General Cambron takes the marble steps three at a time.

'Oh, no, you don't.' Sarah stops him at the door. 'Take off your boots, will you? I won't have you fill the house with sand!'

General Cambron takes off his boots and remains in his stockinged feet, like all the marshals in the hall.

'If I had a maid, I wouldn't mind,' Sarah remarked, 'but she left me the day before yesterday. I told Napoleon that I didn't like her face, but for him anything is more important than his home. Now I'm here without a maid for the weekend, and because of your silly battle I haven't even got time to look for a new one. If you hear of a decent girl who can cook and is willing to take care of the kid, tell me, please, but not a Corsican, if possible, because they talk such a lot.'

'Certainly, Your Imperial Highness.' General Cambron saluted and handed the Emperor an urgent message.

Napoleon looked at it and blanched.

'Gentlemen,' he whispered, 'Fouchet, whom I appointed

Minister of Police, has joined the enemy. What shall we do?'

'Come and eat,' Sarah proposed. 'Everything is getting cold on the table.'

The Empress went into the next room to put the breakfast on the stove again. Napoleon gave his final instructions.

'The world's fate will be decided *here*!' He pointed briskly at the map. 'If the main attack is from the southeast, we'll regroup on the flanks – '

'Napoleon!' It came from the other room. 'Do you want your eggs soft or scrambled?'

'As you like.'

'Scrambled?'

'Yes.'

'Then say so.'

The Eagle pulled on his high boots and put on his cocked hat. His face expressed an iron will to win the Battle of Nations.

'Gentlemen, for France!'

'For France!' the marshals thundered with drawn swords. 'For the Emperor!'

'Napoleon.' Sarah stuck her head through the door. 'The child is calling you.'

'Your Imperial Highness,' Marshal Murat whispered, 'the enemy's at the gate!'

'It's me who'll stay all day long with the crying kid, not you, sir!' Sarah replied. 'It's quite all right for Napoleon to give his son a kiss before he leaves the house.'

'Where's the Aiglon?'

'He's peeing.'

The Emperor left at a run for the other room.

'I've got no maid,' Sarah explained. 'How can I take care of three floors all by myself? I asked you a thousand times not to scatter ash on the rugs. I've only got two hands.'

Napoleon strode with long steps towards the exit.

'What shall I tell them should somebody be looking for you?' Sarah asked.

'Tell them I'm at the Battle of Waterloo.'

'When will you be back?'

'Don't know.'

'I must tell them something, mustn't I? I hope you'll be home for lunch.'

'If I can make it.'

'What would you like to eat?'

'Anything.'

'Stuffed gooseneck?'

'Yes.'

'Then say so.'

The Emperor left.

'You didn't finish your breakfast!' Sarah shouted after him through the window. 'Get me a maid! And don't be late!'

The Emperor's noble figure grew smaller as he advanced through the narrow ravine which led to the fields of Waterloo. Sarah bent down and started sweeping up the sand which the military had brought in. She was all by herself, without a maid. The smell of gunpowder wafted in through the open window, the flashes of cannon could be seen all around. It was then that the armies of Blücher and Wellington at last succeeded in closing their pincers. The two victors – according to the history books – had gone into battle, leaving their faithful wives far behind in the rear.

The Israeli film industry is developing with midget steps. One has to admit that it is hard to practise the Seventh Art in a country so small that spectators have to see every film at least three times to make it worthwhile for the producers. What's more, spectators now and then even have to take parts if they are captured on location.

Continuity

On that fateful early morning I jumped out of bed, awakened by suspicious noises coming from my study, and indeed someone was standing outside on the balcony, knocking on the windowpane. It was be-pyjamaed Morris Kalaniot, my upstairs neighbour.

'Hide me,' he panted, 'hide me!'

'What's happened, Mr Kalaniot?'

'I'm in continuity!'

The man's whole body was shaking, he dragged his left leg and a mute fear flickered in his eyes. I gave him some lukewarm water from the tap and that calmed him somewhat. He kept looking apprehensively upward towards his apartment, from which he had climbed down, and in a choking voice related his tale of woe, which, as a matter of fact, is simply the story of an ordinary film career.

'On that evening I worked late at the office, because the boss had asked me to rewrite some invoices. At about nine o'clock I left for home on foot. Then, next to a house, I saw a big crowd milling around, reflectors and all sorts of cranes. In short: they were shooting a new Israeli film on the staircase. One could hardly see anything because two half-naked wrestlers were standing there pushing back the crowd with merciless blows. Standing next to the camera there was a young man in a singlet, and I realized right away that he was the director, because he kept shouting all the time. The well-known actor Shlomo Emmanueli was also sitting there in an armchair, combing a saucy lock down into his eyes.

'And then suddenly,' Morris went on, 'the director looked round him and shouted: "Damn it, I need another mug in the background!" You have to know that whenever the director says anything, everybody jumps to it. Maybe they aren't doing anything else besides, but they do a lot of jumping. This time one of the director's assistants jumped and turned to the crowd: "Who wants to have his picture taken, boys?" People started pushing like maniacs, I was literally ashamed. The assistants chose me. "Just a few minutes," he said. "Atta boy!"

'I'd never been on a real film set,' my neighbour allowed. 'To tell the truth, I always thought it was like at the theatre – that is, that the whole film was shot at a go, in a matter of two or three hours. I never imagined it was such an elaborate confidence trick. But, I said to myself, it won't hurt you if they see you in the movies. I won't tell a thing to the wife, and suddenly I'll be there on the screen! I asked the assistant whether I'd have to change my looks, get a new hairdo, moustache or something, and then the director started roaring, would I shut up and stand where I was told to stand! What I did was in fact quite easy! I was supposed to stand in a doorway and then Shlomo Emmanueli comes and pushes me aside and shouts: "Taxi! Taxi!"

'They all envied me, naturally, for getting the part, but I couldn't care less. Everybody has to take his chance nowadays, right? The wrestlers – who, by the way, are called "grips" – lifted me up bodily and placed me in a chalk circle. I had to stand exactly within the circle because, according to the story, Shlomo Emmanueli steps on my corns during the "taxi-taxi". It hurt a little, but one has to suffer for art, I read somewhere. We had five painful rehearsals and then the director shouted. "Action!" and they clicked the little black board in front of my nose and shot me in earnest. But in the middle of the shooting the director suddenly shouted: "Cut!" and added: "Tell that idiot not to look into the camera!" I said: "No one told me it was forbidden, really." The assistant asked, meaning me: "Should I kick him out, sir?" but the director replied that anyway they're all half-wits, so what's the use.

'After the first take I wanted to go home,' Morris Kalaniot

continued. 'You long all your life to be in the limelight, and when you finally make it, you find yourself hot under the collar. Besides, in films you do everything at least twenty times before the director says "Print", which means "Not bad". What bothered me most – there was there a be-spectacled young man, "the script girl", whose duty it is to watch things, and he wouldn't let me change feet, and so they stepped eleven times on my left foot and I shouted each time, "Oy!" In general, they keep an iron discipline during shooting. For instance, a man tried desperately to cross over and get into the house in front of which we were shooting. Don't ask me what a dressing down he got from the director: "Get the hell out of here, you limp dishrag," he roared at him, "we are shooting!" The man claimed that he lived in the house and wanted to go to bed. "Go to a hotel," he was told, "you are disturbing us!" They let me go at two thirty that night. I must have been good, because the assistant took down my address and let me take a bite out of a piece of cheese he found lying on one of the cases. My wife said I had been stupid: you get at least a thousand dollars a day for playing in films. But I'm not a real star, my dear, I replied to her, who knows when I'll again play in films?

'Next morning at six I was again in films,' my neighbour sighed. 'At five o'clock there was a ring at the door – you know, one of those long rings when you don't take your finger off the bell – and the two grips invaded my apartment. One of them grabbed me, while the other picked up my clothes, and then we were bundled into a taxi waiting down-stairs. "The director needs you!" they told me as I put on my clothes in the taxi. We were racing like mad, because when they are turning a movie you can't waste even a second: every hour costs at least IL2,000, every minute IL333.33 and every second IL5.55. In other words, if the director sneezes twice, that's a loss equivalent to my monthly salary. When we ar-rived, I told the assistant director that I was in a hurry to get to the office. "What do you mean, you are in a hurry?" the assistant roared at me. "Man, you are in continuity!"

'That's when I first met that word. It means that if you are shot once, from that moment on you must be shot all the time, otherwise there is no continuity and the film can't be cut. Thus, for instance, in my scene I am standing in the background when Shlomo Emmanueli says "Taxi-taxi", so from now on I cannot be replaced in the film because the spectators will say: "Hey, Kalaniot is not in the back! A moment ago he was still there!" See what I mean? That's why they called me again. The director decided to take a close-up shot of Shlomo Emmanueli and I'm to be seen in the background all the time. We made about eight takes and the big toe of my left foot got swollen out of all proportion. And then the script girl suddenly started shouting hysterically: "Stop! Stop! The miserable creep is in a different shirt!"

'The director almost killed me. "Idiot!" he shouted. "You spoiled two hours' shooting!" I protested that no one had told me I had to come in the same shirt as yesterday. My wife lays out on a chair every night fresh clothes, I explained, she doesn't know a thing about continuity. "Shirt!" the director hissed, purple in the face. "Shirt!" They pushed me into a taxi and we rushed home and overturned the laundry basket, but it seems that my wife had already sent the shirt to the laundry. We burst into the laundry, stopped the machines and pulled out the wet shirt. I put it on, and then they dried me in front of a twenty-five-thousand-watt klieg light. "Water," I implored them, "water!" "Oh, yeah," the director sneered. "Murder!"

'We made fourteen takes. Fourteen times Shlomo Emmanueli shouted, "Taxi, taxi", and fourteen times he stepped on my toes. They also shaved the left side of my face, because it showed in the pictures. That was again a matter of continuity: I had been shaven the day before, so I had to be shaven this day as well. I reached the office at three p.m. I told the boss a truck had run over me, and he said I looked it. I fell asleep at once over the ledgers and was awakened by my shouting: "Action! Action!" The boss said he didn't like it.

'Next morning I was working at the office when I heard a familiar noise outside. "Hey!" the grips were shouting in the lobby. "Where are you, hey?" They again took me prisoner.

'They dragged me out in full view of my boss: "The director

needs me," I explained to him from the doorway. In the taxi they stuffed me into the original shirt, which they had previously kidnapped from my home. "We're making a reaction shot," the assistant explained. "We'll show your face contorted with pain as they step on your toes." There was action and I shouted. The director was furious. "You call this shouting?" he asked. "Let him have it with a hammer!" Nine times they dropped a hammer on what was left of my left foot before the results were artistically satisfactory. By eleven a.m. they were through with me. "Out!" the director roared. "Beat it!"

'My boss warned me,' Morris Kalaniot lamented, 'that this was the last time he would tolerate such behaviour. I tried to explain to him that I was at present in a difficult period of continuity, but he had no feeling for show business. In addition to that, at four o'clock I again heard the heavy steps outside. I fled straight into the toilet and locked myself in. They broke down the door without a moment's hesitation and dragged me into the taxi. The boss shouted after me through the window that I needn't bother to come back. It seems that my voice had to be re-recorded because yesterday there had been too many street noises. This is called "post-sync". They placed a microphone in front of my mouth and I shouted "Oy!" every time the hammer hit, I thought quite naturally, but the director thought I was still half asleep and called for a sledgehammer. He hated me immensely and I dared not open my mouth because I was afraid he wouldn't ever take me again. In the middle of the eleventh take I also got a coughing fit and coughed away about IL200 in cash. "He'll be my death, this degenerate!" the director cursed me. "Action!" I finished at midnight, out of breath, out of a job and almost out of a toe. The director personally chased me away with a long stick. "Take this affliction off my back!" he roared. "I don't ever again want to see him!" But altogether it had been a nice experience.'

My neighbour looked upwards and dropped his voice to a whisper:

'Last night I dreamed that they were again taking me for the continuity. And do you think they didn't come? They knocked at the door. "He needs you," they shouted, "for a retake!" That is, one of the shots made yesterday or the day before yesterday – I don't know for sure, I've completely lost any sense of time – was not quite up to scratch and had to be remade. We movie people call this retake. The wife opened the door and told my persecutors that I had died last night. "Never mind," the grips said, "he's only in the background. We'll tie him to a board. Where is the body?" But by then I was outside, sliding down the drainpipe to your balcony. Hide me, for heaven's sake. They're looking for me . . . all over the house.'

Morris fell silent and listened tensely.

From the stairway one could hear heavy steps approaching. . . .

By the way, Morris is not in the picture, they cut out the whole scene.

Our youth, apples of our eyes, sweet native-born kids, are six feet two inches in the shade and their attitude to their fathers is definitely parental. In our schools, corporal punishment has been introduced long ago: otherwise how could one cope with the teachers?

Good-bye Mr Chips

September 13. Today I started my pedagogical career at an elementary school, where I am replacing a fugitive teacher. Wonderful feeling, to have a roomful of sweet and lively sabras hanging on your every word.

The first lesson began most auspiciously. But somewhat later – after about a minute, that is – a pupil in the first row called Zatopek turned on his transistor. I warned him three times that I wouldn't tolerate light music in class. In the end I lost my temper and ordered him out.

'You get out!' Zatopek replied and went on fiddling with the knobs in search of pop music on shortwave. I hurried down to the headmaster. He warned me that under no circumstances ought I to leave the classroom. 'If one of you has to get out, it certainly must be him!' the headmaster opined. 'Never show signs of weakness!' I returned to class and demonstratively lectured on the Song of Deborah. But I am sure that Zatopek nurses a grudge against me.

September 27. There has been a rather unpleasant incident. We don't yet know for certain who is to blame. As far as I can remember, the scuffle started after I spotted a spelling error in Zatopek's essay. In the sentence 'We are crazy about Bible studies' the boy had misspelled the first word as 'Ve'. I stood behind Zatopek while he was writing and pointed out this serious error to him. Thereupon he seized a ruler and hit me across the fingers. It hurt! I am not a champion of blind discipline in our educational system, and I reject corporal punishment as a pedagogical means. I immediately asked the errant student to send me his parents, and complained to the headmaster.

'According to Ottoman Law, a pupil may hit his teacher, but the teacher may not hit back,' the headmaster explained. 'Don't get too near them.'

September 28. This morning Zatopek's parents dropped in: the mother, two fathers and a number of uncles. 'So my boy is an idiot?' one of the fathers roared. 'My boy can't write, hey?' There followed a brief but stormy exchange of blows and then they tried to push me against the wall, but I was not impressed and nimbly slipped between their legs and locked myself in the headmaster's room. The parents battered on the door.

'They'll break it down in a minute,' the frightened headmaster whispered. 'Better surrender yourself.'

I explained to him that this would inevitably tarnish my father image in the students' eyes. The boys dragged some benches into the corridor and lined up along the wall to have a better view, cheering on the Zatopeks.

Luckily, an inspector of the Ministry of Education arrived and enforced a truce. According to the compromise agreed on through his mediation, Zatopek's parents evacuated the building, and ve shall no longer meddle with the students' spelling.

October 9. Today's demonstrations were particularly rowdy. About a dozen seventh-form students milled about the barbed-wire fence thrown up around the school building, and somewhat later burned me in effigy. I realized that matters had got out of hand and went to consult the headmaster.

'You see, these are the ways of our fighting, pioneering youth,' the veteran pedagogue explained. 'They were born in a free country, they are sons of the desert. They utterly lack inferiority complexes. You cannot get through to them with conventional scolding and punishments. They appreciate only bullies of Matuska's sort.'

Matuska is our PT teacher, a pleasant fellow weighing two hundred pounds. Strangely enough, at his lessons there reigns complete silence and order, and it seems that the pupils' parents do not bother him with complaints. I asked the headmaster what was Matuska's secret.

'He's simply a pedagogue,' the headmaster said. 'He never touches his pupils. He only kicks them.'

I started taking judo lessons at a gymnasium. In my group of twelve all were teachers. I made up my mind to hit back. The headmaster does not yet know about this.

October 21. Our trade union informed us that the Minister of Finance was dead set against special 'danger pay' for teachers because, in his view, so far there has been no open fighting on the educational front. That's a pity. I owe money to everybody: the grocer, the insurance man and also the lawyer who is drawing up my will. Because I have decided to fail Zatopek in grammar.

Half my fortune, IL25 in cash, I willed to the hostel for paralysed teachers and to widows whose husbands fell on the field of education in the line of duty. I informed the headmaster that yesterday they had shot at me from a rooftop. He advised me to stay indoors until after the exams.

Anyway, I failed Zatopek.

October 22. I had clean forgotten that Zatopek's brother was a sergeant major in the Artillery. The bombardment started in the morning while we were discussing Herzl's vision. We hurried down into the shelter built a few years ago after the son of an Air Force pilot had flunked his math course. About twenty shells exploded nearby.

Around noon the director went out with a white flag and brought back the rebels' terms:

' "Fair" in grammar and an apology.'

Only the right wing of the school was damaged. The students were not satisfied with my apologies (which they said were not sincere) and took the headmaster as a hostage. I phoned the Minister of Education and protested against the humiliations we teachers have to endure. How can we serve as a model to our pupils if we must always walk in pairs lest they jump at us from behind? It is a question of professional dignity. A headmaster who is slapped every day loses face. The Minister promised to look into the matter, but at the same time warned us against further blackmail.

November 15. What I have dreaded all the time has happened. Zatopek caught a cold. This morning a posse of policemen came to the school and arrested me, as the boy had denounced me for criminal negligence. In vain did I assure them that it was not I who had left the window open. Zatopek's family unanimously testified against me. The representative of the Red Cross asked whether I had any request before the trial.

I mused as I was lying on my cot. 'The solution to Israel's educational problems,' I muttered, 'is remote control ... the teacher must be removed as far as possible from his pupils ... far ... far ... way up there ... like a highest authority ... a sort of god ... but how ...?'

November 16 A miracle has happened. I opened the newspaper and ...

We are no longer in danger of our lives.

Educational TV is on its way.

In the nick of time.

Our society is continually progressing with giant steps towards the total blending of the diasporas. The deep differences between the Oriental immigrant and the newcomer from Europe, which only a few years ago looked unbridgeable, are now taken for granted. But in the meantime a new generation has arisen that likes its food just as hot and spicy.

A Matter of Porterage

Cast: Sa'adia Shabetai, our Oriental friend
Mr Pollack, the exact opposite of Shabetai
Scene: In front of the entrance to the house in which Mr Pollack is living

POLLACK (*enters from the side and shouts directions to someone still in the wings*): That's it ... that's it ... this way, old boy ... easy ... yes ...

SA'ADIA (*enters staggering under the weight of a big armchair*)

POLLACK: Here we are, old boy. Now up those stairs, carefully ... third floor, apartment No. 4, Pollack.

SA'ADIA (*lowers armchair to sidewalk*)

POLLACK (*impatient*): Come on, old boy, let's not waste any more time. Grab that armchair and let's go.

SA'ADIA (*pulls out of his pocket a small tin box and with Olympian calm starts rolling a cigarette*)

POLLACK: Come on, old boy, come on. We lost enough time on the way here. Pick it up, old boy, and let's go.

SA'ADIA (*spits out tobacco leaves which stuck to his tongue*)

POLLACK (*gradually losing his self-confidence*): Please ... really ... just haul it up that flight of stairs, old boy ... there's nothing to it, really ... old ... boy ...

SA'ADIA: Who, me?

POLLACK: Yes. Carry that armchair up, please.

SA'ADIA: Me? Not me.

POLLACK: What do you mean, not you?

SA'ADIA: Not me.

POLLACK: Now just a moment, old boy. We clearly agreed that you would carry my armchair up to the house.

SA'ADIA: Up to the house? So this is the house. Is this Mr Pollack's house?

POLLACK: Yes.

SA'ADIA (*pointing at spot in front of entrance*): So I got to carry it up to here.

POLLACK: And who will carry it up to my apartment?

SA'ADIA: That I don't know.

POLLACK: What do you mean, you don't know?

SA'ADIA: I don't know what you mean. A house is a house. Upstairs – that's another matter.

POLLACK: No, old boy. Up to the house means up to my living room.

SA'ADIA: That isn't written in the Bible. Only you say so, Mr Pollack.

POLLACK: But we agreed that the eight pounds you got were to be an all-inclusive fee!

SA'ADIA: Inclusive, yes, very inclusive. But a house is a house, and upstairs is upstairs.

POLLACK: You know, old boy, what you are trying to do is blackmail.

SA'ADIA (*does not understand*): Now?

POLLACK: What now?

SA'ADIA: Mr Pollack, this chair is very heavy!

POLLACK: It's an armchair!

SA'ADIA: Armchair. That makes it even heavier.

POLLACK: All right! (*Takes off his coat and steps up to the armchair, muttering*) Gangsters! Their word is worthless, all they care about is how to rob you of your last penny. (*To* SA'ADIA) What are you waiting for?

SA'ADIA: I'm not waiting. I'm just hanging around.

POLLACK: For once, old boy, it won't work! With me it's a principle.

SA'ADIA: Principle?

POLLACK: Principle, old boy. No one ever cheats me. Thank goodness, I've been a sportsman all my life. If you are interested, I can show you a few trophies I have at home.

SA'ADIA: I'm not interested.

POLLACK (*grabs armchair and tries to lift it*): No, old boy, you don't know me. If necessary . . . I'm ready . . . even . . . today . . . at my age . . . (*The armchair won't budge,* POLLACK *gives up, speaks in a more conciliatory voice*) Now really, this is ridiculous. Must we quarrel over a few pennies?

SA'ADIA (*offended*): Pennies? You want pennies, Mr Pollack? I can give you a few if you wish. A house is a house . . .

POLLACK (*roaring*): . . . and upstairs is upstairs!

SA'ADIA: Of course. What floor did you say, Mr Pollack?

POLLACK (*suavely*): Second floor. Very small floors, really.

SA'ADIA: Just a minute. We think. (*After thinking it over*) Why second floor, all of a sudden? You said third floor before, Mr Pollack.

POLLACK: All right, third floor. What difference does it make.

SA'ADIA: It makes one hell of a difference. For second floor I charge three pounds. For third floor – only two.

POLLACK: Why?

SA'ADIA: It's a principle, Mr Pollack. On the second floor, apartments are more expensive because there live people with plenty of money. From the third floor I don't take so much, because there live people with less money.

POLLACK: All right, that will do. This armchair still has to go up there. (*Again tries to lift the armchair*) Half a pound?

SA'ADIA: Half a pound for up these? No, Mr Pollack. For half a pound I'll only put the chair on your back.

POLLACK: This is an armchair!

SA'ADIA: All right, the armchair.

POLLACK (*furious*): O.K. (*Bends down*) Let's go!

SA'ADIA (*lifts armchair, prepares to put it on Pollack's back*): Mr Pollack is right, so help me he's right. He'll keep his money and also make sport for the trophies. (*Straining all his muscles, as if the armchair were terribly heavy*) Are you in a Sick Fund, Mr Pollack?

POLLACK (*still bent*): Of course.

SA'ADIA: That's good. At least you'll get free treatment, Mr Pollack.

POLLACK (*suddenly straightens*): A pound!

SA'ADIA: One pound?

POLLACK: One pound.

SA'ADIA: For up there?

POLLACK: For the kangaroo at the zoo!

SA'ADIA: I don't want no kangaroo. Finished! (*Prepares to go*)

POLLACK (*runs after him*): Why are you so stubborn, old boy? Come, let's compromise.

SA'ADIA: Nothing doing, Mr Pollack. I got no time for you. For up there I get three pounds and that's that.

POLLACK: But I already gave you half a pound.

SA'ADIA: All right, so three and a half pounds. It doesn't matter.

POLLACK: Listen, my dear boy. . . . What's your name?

SA'ADIA: Three and a half, Mr Pollack, and basta.

POLLACK: I asked, what's your name?

SA'ADIA: My name? Sa'adia. Sa'adia Shabetai.

POLLACK: So listen, Mr Shabetai, you have to put it in your thick skull that in this country, you hear, in this country it won't do to be too smart. You can cheat a man only once.

SA'ADIA: Once?

POLLACK: Yes, once. But that is the end of your career! If you want to get work in the future as well . . .

SA'ADIA: But I don't. You can't work all the time.

POLLACK: No, no, Mr Shabetai, that's not the way. You are new in this country. . . .

SA'ADIA: Abroad it was much better. I don't like it here.

POLLACK: You are still new in this country, Mr Shabetai, you have to be modest, not exaggerate in your demands, follow the golden rule. . . .

SA'ADIA (*suddenly losing his temper*): Gold? Three and a half pounds are gold?

POLLACK: That isn't what I meant, Mr Shabetai. I only wanted to say that we have to come to an agreement.

SA'ADIA: And how much is that worth to you?

POLLACK: Mr Sa'adia, what are we actually quarrelling about? It's quite simple, really: you are asking three and a half pounds and I'm offering one pound. Let's meet midway.

SA'ADIA: Where?

POLLACK: Let's make a fair compromise, Mr Shabetai, the way honest people do.

SA'ADIA: All right. Just a minute, we think. . . . (*After thinking it over*) I'll make you a compromise, Mr Pollack, but that's my last word, so help me.

POLLACK: All right. How much do you want?

SA'ADIA: Three and a half pounds.

POLLACK: All right! All right! But this is your last price, your gross price, I hope!

SA'ADIA: Gross? Why gross? This is a very heavy chair, very heavy.

POLLACK: Armchair!

SA'ADIA: I can feel my whole body going to pieces under its weight – and you call it gross?

POLLACK (*resignedly*): O.K., not gross.

SA'ADIA: So why does Mr Pollack say gross?

POLLACK: I didn't say a thing. Forget it, Mr Shabetai, for God's sake. Take that armchair and let's go.

SA'ADIA: Got a cigarette, Mr Pollack?

POLLACK (*holds out packet*): Here.

SA'ADIA: Thanks. (*Takes whole packet*) Fine cigarettes. What's your job, Mr Pollack?

POLLACK: I'm a bookkeeper.

SA'ADIA: Ah, horseracing!

POLLACK: No, no, I'm a government official, old boy.

SA'ADIA: A government official?

POLLACK: Yes.

SA'ADIA (*lets go of armchair*): Then I get another half a pound.

POLLACK: Another half a pound?

SA'ADIA: Yes. A tip.

POLLACK: And what about the three and a half pounds?

SA'ADIA: That's my fee. The half-pound is a tip. And don't try to haggle, Mr Pollack. I like officials the way I like Asian flu. They pay the most, because they make me queue up for hours on end. (*Puts out his hand*) Four pounds and that's that.

POLLACK (*utterly frustrated*): Listen, old boy, enough is

enough! There's a limit even to my patience! I'd rather have this chair –

SA'ADIA: Armchair!

POLLACK: – this armchair rot here in front of the house than submit to any more of your blackmail!

SA'ADIA (*looking up at the sky*): It's going to rain.

POLLACK: I don't care. You aren't going to grow rich at my expense!

SA'ADIA (*deeply offended*): Grow rich? Who wants to grow rich? For vegetables you pay every day more, Mr Pollack, but that's all right, eh? That's the government! But when Sa'adia Shabetai, who's got only one pair of pants, ups his fee a little bit for extra-heavy work, he's growing rich, eh?

POLLACK: All right, so you don't grow rich.

SA'ADIA: What do you think, Mr Pollack, how many armchairs a week do I get?

POLLACK: I don't know, old boy.

SA'ADIA: One, Mr Pollock, just one! So one has to get a little money out of it, to make ends meet, doesn't one? Listen: one has to eat, yes? One needs kerosene for the burner, yes? Sixty piastres, you hear, sixty piastres a month one needs just for Habuba's kindergarten! And a comforter for little Mordechai one also needs!

POLLACK: All right, Mr Shabetai, all right . . .

SA'ADIA: What do you mean, all right? If you, Mr Pollack, had as many troubles as I have, you would ask a hundred pounds for carrying this chair up those stairs. What do you think? Electricity one needs, yes? Teeth for the wife, she needs? A coat for Mazal one needs, yes? A doctor for the ring Simeon swallowed one needs, yes?

POLLACK: One needs . . . one needs . . .

SA'ADIA: Why does one need? Who needs a doctor? The wife leaves Simeon alone for a minute, so the boy takes the wife's ring and eats it.

POLLACK: Good Lord!

SA'ADIA: It was the nicest ring in the whole neighbourhood, Mr Pollack. The wife had gotten it from her mother. We were scared to death. I said to the doctor: 'Doc, if you don't take out this ring I'll start a sit-down strike at the Jewish Agency.'

POLLACK: But in the end did you find it?

SA'ADIA: Yes. But Simeon had eaten one of its stones. The snotty brat. We threw a big party, Mr Pollack. The whole family filled up on shishkebab.

POLLACK: With hot peppers?

SA'ADIA: No, Mr Pollack! With bandjan kebabi.

POLLACK: And plates of phull, I hope.

SA'ADIA: Of course. Without phull it's worthless. (*Suddenly realizes what* POLLACK *is saying*) Mr Pollack . . . Mr Pollack . . . you know Oriental dishes?

POLLACK: Unfortunately. That's all I get to eat, day after day.

SA'ADIA: At home?

POLLACK: At home.

SA'ADIA: And who cooks those things for you, Mr Pollack?

POLLACK: Who? My wife, of course.

SA'ADIA: Mr Pollack's wife?

POLLACK: Uhum.

SA'ADIA: What's the name of Mr Pollack's wife?

POLLACK: What business is that of yours?

SA'ADIA: It is my business.

POLLACK: Allegra.

SA'ADIA: Allegra?

POLLACK: Allegra.

SA'ADIA: That's not a European name.

POLLACK: Did I say she was European?

SA'ADIA: So you say, Mr Pollack, that your wife's name is Allegra?

POLLACK: So what?

SA'ADIA: And Allegra cooks Mr Pollack our dishes? Mahshi kussa?

POLLACK: Mahshi kussa? Are you kidding? She cooks Mahshi shekal with rezi fasulya!

SA'ADIA (*beaming*): No, Mr Pollack!

POLLACK: So help me.

SA'ADIA: Any children?

POLLACK: Yes, one, David. (*Pulls out photo*)

SA'ADIA (*examines it*): Nice kid, David, though a little swarthy. What do you eat on Saturdays, Mr Pollack?

POLLACK: On Saturdays? Lahman shwaye.

SA'ADIA: That's good.

POLLACK: You can have it. My whole mouth is on fire for days after it.

SA'ADIA: Never mind, Mr Pollack. Sure, it burns a little bit, but it gives you lots of strength.

POLLACK: Nonsense! Ruba kemia always upsets my stomach.

SA'ADIA (*radiant*): Upsets? Really? Eat it with a little burghul, Mr Pollack, then it won't be so hot. Tell Allegra not to put in so much filful, just some bandjan and a dash of basil.

POLLACK: All right.

SA'ADIA: Allegra – that's an Oriental name, isn't it?

POLLACK: I told you it is.

SA'ADIA: Good boy. And what else upsets Mr Pollack's stomach?

POLLACK: Kuba nabulsia is even worse.

SA'ADIA: Kuba nabulsia? (*Enthusiastically*) I'm telling you Mr Pollack, if you'll eat lots of kuba nabulsia, you'll have as much gross strength as Ben-Gurion and you'll be able to carry ten armchairs on your head. Like this: watch! (*Lifts armchair as if it were feather-light*) But still, dajaj mookli is the best, isn't it, Mr Pollack?

POLLACK: If the meat is well done. (*Puts hand in his pocket*) All right, here is your money, old boy.

SA'ADIA: What money?

POLLACK: For carrying the armchair up there.

SA'ADIA: What up there? Those few steps up there? What do you take me for, Mr Pollack? (*Exit with armchair*)

CURTAIN

More about Penguins

Penguinews, which appears every month, contains details of all the new books issued by Penguins as they are published. From time to time it is supplemented by *Penguins in Print*, which is a complete list of all books published by Penguins which are in print. (There are well over three thousand of these.)

A specimen copy of *Penguinews* will be sent to you free on request, and you can become a subscriber for the price of the postage. For a year's issues (including the complete lists) please send 4s. if you live in the United Kingdom, or 8s. if you live elsewhere. Just write to Dept EP, Penguin Books Ltd, Harmondsworth, Middlesex, enclosing a cheque or postal order, and your name will be added to the mailing list.

Some other books published by Penguins are described on the following page.

Note: *Penguinews* and *Penguins in Print* are not available in the U.S.A. or Canada

A Soldier's Diary Sinai 1967

Yael Dayan

The war that nobody wanted happened, and Yael Dayan was there to record it – with compassion, drama and her own unique poetic sense. Not as an outsider, sent to report on someone else's nightmare, but as an Israeli by birth, Yael Dayan, daughter of the victorious general, reflects the passion, the desperation and the triumph of her entire country.

A Soldier's Diary is a day-by-day account of her experiences in combat '. . . talking, explaining and strengthening the pride of this extraordinary army which is bound to win'.

Not for sale in the U.S.A.

Look Back, Mrs Lot!

Ephraim Kishon

Look Back, Mrs Lot! – a book that is as easy to bite into as a Jaffa orange – is the first to be published in English by the writer who is regarded as Israel's top humorist.

In this composite picture of Canaan as she is, Ephraim Kishon whips the Zionist filter off the lens, and lo! the land flowing with milk, honey, and American parcels lies before our dazzled eyes. A land of muddles and miracles, where anything can happen, and usually does; a land where the party is the ladder to success; a land where they're determined to rebuild the Tower of Babel.